THE
GLOBAL-WARMING
DECEPTION

THE
GLOBAL-WARMING
DECEPTION

How a Secret Elite Plans to
Bankrupt America and Steal Your Freedom

GRANT R. JEFFREY

BEST-SELLING AUTHOR OF *THE NEXT WORLD WAR*

WATERBROOK
PRESS

The Global-Warming Deception
Published by WaterBrook Press
12265 Oracle Boulevard, Suite 200
Colorado Springs, Colorado 80921

ISBN 978-1-4000-7443-3
ISBN 978-0-307-72940-8 (electronic)

Published in the United States by WaterBrook Multnomah, an imprint of the Crown Publishing Group, a division of Random House Inc., New York.

WaterBrook and its deer colophon are registered trademarks of Random House Inc.

Library of Congress Cataloging-in-Publication Data
Jeffrey, Grant R.
    The global-warming deception : how a secret elite plans to bankrupt America and steal your freedom / Grant R. Jeffrey.—1st ed.
        p. cm.
Includes bibliographical references.
    ISBN 978-1-4000-7443-3—ISBN 978-0-307-72940-8 (electronic)
1. Global warming—Religious aspects—Christianity. 2. Christianity and politics—United States. 3. United States—Church history—21st century. 4. Elite (Social sciences)—Political activity—United States—History—21st century. I. Title.
    BR517.J44 2011
    261.8—dc22

                                                        2010043660

2011—First Edition

CONTENTS

INTRODUCTION

The ultimate message of Bible prophecy is not one of doom and gloom, but rather the hope of redemption when Christ returns. The Church and the earth itself will be redeemed by Jesus Christ, the Lord of the universe. We have this sure promise in the person and completed work of Jesus. The redemption of humanity and the earth will take place in our generation, with the return of Christ to set up His Kingdom.

In *The Global-Warming Deception,* we will look at the anthropogenic global warming (AGW) movement in light of God's truth as it is revealed in the Scriptures. We will examine the hidden, sinister political agenda of an elite group that uses supposedly legitimate nongovernmental organizations (NGOs) to advance its own interests. We will also look at a large number of taxpayer-funded groups that help advance a diabolical environmental agenda.

Why is so much of the globalist agenda hidden from public view? On the surface of things, it would seem that organized efforts to combat global warming should result in benefits for all of us. Who wants to see temperatures increase to the point that glaciers and icecaps melt, flooding coastal regions and allowing salt water to contaminate a good portion of the world's supply of fresh water? Who would want to see average global temperatures rise so high that significant plant and animal life are threatened, and humanity is forced to develop new technologies just to enable humans to survive in an increasingly hostile environment?

No one wants that to occur. And if the highly publicized environmental dangers were based on certain scientific fact, we would be foolish if we failed to combat the threat with every resource we have. But does hard science back up the widely accepted claim that human activity—primarily related to the use of fossil fuels—is the major cause of global warming? And has unbiased science fully documented a rise in average global temperatures? These are a few of the crucial questions that will be answered in the chapters that follow.

I have been a committed environmentalist since I was a teenager. I have long embraced conservation of the earth's species and habitat as a biblically supported principle. When I joined Abitibi Paper Company at its Toronto, Canada, headquarters in 1968, I not only supported recycling of paper at our Thorald paper mill, but I assisted in the creation of the recycling symbol (the mobius strip) to depict our commitment to utilize recycled paper as part of an environmental program that was still in its infancy. Variations of this recycling symbol were developed in numerous nations and are now used globally.

Preservation of the environment is a biblical mandate for all Christians and Jews who treasure the Word of God. However, we must also protect our Judeo-Christian values, which are under attack from radical environmentalists who seek to destroy the fundamental principles of Western civilization.

With the fall of the Soviet Union and the Soviet Eastern bloc in the late twentieth century, powerful socialistic forces began looking for a new strategy to use in establishing a global, totalitarian, socialist regime. Communism and socialism had been proven politically and economically bankrupt. Even Communist China is now thriving with a heavily regulated and limited form of capitalism under totalitarian political control. The world has become a very different place since Mikhail Gorbachev dismantled the Soviet Communist Party, leading to the dissolution of the USSR in 1990–91.

Most of the formerly Communist nations (except North Korea and Cuba) have either rejected the discredited system outright or have adapted it, as is the case with China, to take advantage of the overwhelming economic benefits of capitalism. The globalist elite, while not abandoning their socialist-Marxist goals, have taken a more devious approach. They came up with a political strategy that is far easier to sell to the general public, news media, educators, and national governments. Their new strategy has been working extremely well in influencing public opinion and attracting massive public support. Without revealing their ultimate goal, the globalist elite have been transforming the regulations, laws, economies, and societies of the world.

In this book we will examine the dark soul and hidden motivations of the AGW movement. The international effort to "save" humanity from the proclaimed future threat of an unbearably warm climate is built on lies, manipulated research, the destruction of historical temperature data, and the intimidation and silencing of climate-change critics. The movement's goals are imposed on sovereign nations by means of binding, unendorsed international treaties. We will weigh the evidence that demonstrates that almost everything we have been told about humanity's contributions to global warming is a deliberate distortion of the facts.

The global-warming deception is so effective because it is based on a partial truth. As we often read in Scripture, when Satan deceives a person, he uses a partial or twisted truth to bait the trap. In just about every instance, save Satan's quoting of Scripture to Jesus in the desert, Satan was successful in his deception. The serpent twisted the words of God in the garden to deceive Eve and left all of humanity with the tragic inheritance of sin. Satan has used minor doctrinal differences, with both sides arguing against the other based on Scripture, throughout church history to divide Christians and to split churches. Satan masquerades as an "angel of light" to deceive as many as possible: "And no marvel; for Satan himself is transformed into an angel of light" (2 Corinthians 11:14).

We see the same pattern in the machinations of the globalist elite, as they seize upon an outwardly noble cause to protect the environment. They begin with the truth: With population growth and increased industrialization in China, India, and other developing nations, humanity is increasing its reliance on fossil fuels. Inevitably we are contributing more and more carbon dioxide (CO_2) every year to the atmosphere. A skilled deceiver always begins with the truth.

Global-warming alarmists, including former vice president Al Gore and the United Nations Intergovernmental Panel on Climate Change (IPCC), point out that the level of CO_2 in the atmosphere has increased annually since the 1860s Civil War. The continued growth in the world economy (especially China's and India's) will accelerate the rate of increase of the level of CO_2 in the atmosphere.

Now for the lie and the imposed guilt that comes with it. After displaying a graph illustrating rising levels of CO_2, the champions of limiting AGW turn to another graph illustrating the pattern of rising global temperature during the same period of time. The implication is clear: as the level of CO_2 rises, the level of global temperature will inexorably rise as well. *However, there is no consistent, peer-reviewed scientific research that establishes a cause-and-effect relationship between increased atmospheric CO_2 and higher global temperatures.*

It's a clever deception, but a lie nonetheless. The AGW hoax lacks any basis in independently verifiable science. It is built on a grain of truth and a well-formed foundation of exaggeration, deliberate deception, and strong-arm tactics to promote the AGW view with educators and media.

In many cases, it is well-meaning environmentally focused people who work to prevent the global warming "crisis." They want to spare humanity an uninhabitable world. But they were conscripted into the movement by deliberate lies, and they work unknowingly to advance the agenda of an unseen globalist elite. The organized effort to combat AGW is the tactic chosen by the globalist elite to impose a centralized, worldwide socialist-Marxist government. They have frightened citizens and coerced governments, and so far nothing has stood in their way.

Abraham Lincoln has been credited with numerous statements that may or may not have originated with him. One of his statements reveals a profound human and political truth. He held that people generally have two reasons they use to justify every decision they make. The first is a public reason and it appears logical. But this reason—which is shared with others—is seldom the real underlying, motivating reason for the action taken. The actual underlying reason is hidden and based on emotion. This second reason is the *real* motivating reason for the decision.

Unless we understand a person's second, hidden reason, we will never understand the true motives behind that person's actions. As you read the documentation in this book, you will realize that those who lead the effort to combat AGW are not primarily motivated to reduce future global temperature increases. Instead, they are bent on forcing the capitalist, free enterprise economies of the West to submit to a global socialist-Marxist government.

Students of Bible prophecy will see many familiar themes throughout this book. Leaders in the AGW movement give us a near-textbook object lesson in implementing the global government agenda in the last days. The great themes of biblical prophecy, the last acts of the powerful story of redemption, the ultimate battle between God and Satan, all of these will take place in our generation. As you read *The Global-Warming Deception*, keep these truths in mind. We are witnessing the unfolding—in public policy, international relations, and false environmental science—of a major tactic being used by Satan to advance his evil agenda on earth. He will ultimately fail, as we know, but prior to his fall he will send his emissary, the Antichrist, to rule the earth as the coming global dictator.

The unprecedented rise of global government in our generation was prophesied by Daniel twenty-five hundred years ago. Daniel warned about the rise of a revived Roman Empire that would be "diverse from all kingdoms, and shall devour the whole earth, and shall tread it down, and break it in pieces" (Daniel 7:23).

The apostle John also warned of the rise of a global dictator, the Antichrist, who would rule the earth in the final seven years of tribulation until he and Satan will be defeated by Jesus Christ at the Battle of Armageddon.

> And I saw the beast, and the kings of the earth, and their armies, gathered together to make war against him [Jesus] that sat on the horse, and against his army. And the beast was taken, and with him the false prophet that wrought miracles before him, with which he deceived them that had received the mark of the beast, and them that worshipped his image. These both were cast alive into a lake of fire burning with brimstone. (Revelation 19:19–20)

We will examine in detail the far-reaching global-warming deception, which is the greatest threat to our nation and our basic liberties and freedoms in our generations, as well as to our standard of living. Our parents and grandparents faced the threat of Nazi Germany, Japanese militarism, and global Communism, and they triumphed. The threat to our fundamental liberties from the global-warming deception is just as dangerous. If we do not awaken to face the hidden socialist and globalist agenda of those who wish to destroy our Judeo-Christian values and democratic freedoms, then the proponents of AGW alarmism will win.

The Hidden Agenda of Global Warming Is Global Government

The biblical prophets described a centralized world government that will gain complete power over all the nations in the last days. Once the "revived Roman Empire" structure is set in place and preliminary work has been done to quell opposition to the global regime, Satan's most accomplished and most powerful servant will appear. The Antichrist will enter the scene as the global dictator, at first with promises of world peace, economic prosperity, and other socialist "spread the wealth" assurances. He will convince the people of the world that he alone can assure their well-being and security. Daniel warns that the Antichrist "shall divide the land for gain" (Daniel 11:39). Satan and the Antichrist are experts at using deception to achieve their goals. Deception is also the preferred method of those leading the anthropogenic global warming (AGW) movement.

The leaders and supporters of the AGW movement have perpetrated an elaborate deception on the citizens, the statesmen, and the nations of the world. A far-reaching global-warming industry has already achieved many of its initial goals. It is given credence by governments, the media, politicians, individual citizens, and much of the scientific community. In less than a quarter century, the environmental movement has grown from spreading the word about the so-called dangers inherent in humanity's impact on climate change to commanding the force of numerous United Nations agencies. Leaders of the AGW movement now have the ability to convene international summits and force nations to violate their own constitutions in signing international climate agreements. These agreements will drastically reduce the standard of living as well as the economic freedom of the citizens of Western democracies.

If you examine the ultimate goals of the globalist groups that determine the strategy and tactics of the global-warming industry, you can't ignore the fact that it is identical to the centralized control of the world that will be in the hands of the prophesied Antichrist. The AGW alarmist camp and the socialist-Marxist elite that pulls the strings will not rest until they achieve global control—politically, socially, economically, and militarily. They will not stop until they have abrogated and nullified national constitutions and your own personal freedoms.

Some of the key scientists in the AGW movement falsify historical temperature data to make it conform to their agenda. The global-warming alarmists silence climate-change critics to avoid public debate over the scientific validity of AGW theory. This is not just poor science, it is a deliberate deception. This systematic fraud can be traced to an international elite that is bent on forcing democratic governments to support a globalist autocracy. The fight against global warming is what they have decided to use for leverage.

Consider the prophet Daniel's description of the Antichrist, the coming leader of the future global government:

> And in the latter time of their kingdom, when the transgressors are come to the full, a king of fierce countenance, and understanding dark sentences, shall stand up.
>
> And his power shall be mighty, but not by his own power: and he shall destroy wonderfully, and shall prosper, and practise, and shall destroy the mighty and the holy people.
>
> And through his policy also he shall cause craft to prosper in his hand; and he shall magnify himself in his heart, and by peace shall destroy many: he shall also stand up against the Prince of princes; but he shall be broken without hand. (8:23–25)

Those who support the AGW alarmists include national government leaders, politicians, scientists, members of the news media, private organizations, multinational companies, and members of the intellectual elite. Their agenda is decidedly anti-Western, antidemocracy, and anticapitalism. The methodology is complex but readily apparent: massive scientific hype and exaggeration, falsification of historical temperature data, and negating well-established scientific data (such as the Medieval Warm Period and the Little Ice Age). Anything that disproves the AGW theory is discounted, silenced, or falsified.

They speak of rapidly melting polar icecaps, the threat of a dramatic rise in sea levels, increasing global temperatures, the destruction of entire species due to climate change, and other environmental "threats" to the survival of humanity—unless we take drastic action to reduce carbon dioxide (CO_2) emissions. The unspoken agenda is to promote fear and dread among citizens (including schoolchildren), politicians, business leaders, and governments. But why do they resort to scare tactics?

The first reason is because fear is an effective motivator, and the news media love scary headlines. Fear sells.

The second reason is because fearful citizens and politicians feel great urgency to "do something!" Fear of global doom can be used to force sovereign nations to accept enormous social and political changes: massive reductions in the quality of life and standard of living, while accepting the burden of massive taxation, with most of the tax revenues going overseas. All this and more simply to respond to a *fabricated and exaggerated* environmental threat. It's not too strong to call this *"international environmental extortion."*

The hidden AGW end game is to weaken and eventually subvert Western free-market economies, sovereign nations, and capitalistic democracies. This will enable the socialist-Marxist elite to take control of commerce, economics, politics, and national governments. Using the false threat of man-made global warming as the wedge, the globalist elite want to impose their full political agenda. They won't stop until they have established an unchallenged global government controlled by an intellectual, scientific, and political elite.

LIVING IN PROPHETIC TIMES

We are living in remarkable times—the most exciting in history. Our era has witnessed tremendous progress in science, medicine, and the proclamation of the gospel of Christ throughout the world. At the same time, we are living in deeply troubling and dangerous times. We need to be in prayer, asking God for clearer spiritual vision, for discernment, and for a fuller knowledge of His truth as revealed in the Scriptures. We are beginning to see more clearly the most dangerous aspects of the AGW movement. The AGW elitists want to use our love for the environment (God's creation) to manipulate us and destroy the fundamental Judeo-Christian political, economic, and spiritual values that form the philosophical foundation of the United States and Canada.

This much is clear from Scripture: The Antichrist will consolidate all political, economic, social, and military power on a scale never before seen on earth. He will rise to rule the world initially through his control of a confederation of ten major European and North African–Mediterranean nations. This will be the fulfillment of the prophesied revival of the ancient Roman Empire, which both Daniel and John foretold (see Daniel 2; Revelation 13). Daniel's visions take on an undeniable sense of urgency for us because he was describing *our own generation.* The prophetic future is now at the door.

The Scriptures warn us of the events that will occur prior to the return of Jesus Christ. The Antichrist and his partner, the False Prophet, will orchestrate the implementation of the Mark of the Beast, a totalitarian police system whereby every person on earth will be tracked during the last three and a half years of the Great Tribulation, prior to the Battle of Armageddon. Those who accept the Mark of the Beast will be free to do business, to work, to make purchases, and to exchange money for services. They will be allowed to lead a semblance of a normal life (see Revelation 13:16–17). But by accepting the mark 666, a person is acknowledging his or her spiritual submission to the Antichrist as "god."

As you read about the AGW movement and its strategies to subvert Western democracies, you will see close parallels to the Bible's descriptions of political and spiritual developments in the last days. It would be easy to feel fearful or anxious in light of the tremendous success of the propagandists and policy makers within the AGW movement. But we need to remember that in all these things, God is the Lord of the universe. He is the sovereign Creator and Sustainer of the world.

God has not left us without hope or without the necessary prophetic revelation of the coming future. He has provided prophetic knowledge in the

Scriptures in advance of the Second Coming. As you study the signs of the end times, thank God that the troubling events in our days are setting the stage for the long-awaited return of Jesus Christ. After the terrible days of the seven-year Tribulation, Christ will return with His resurrected Christians to defeat Satan. At that time, He will establish His millennial rule on earth. He will finally establish the righteous government that humanity has longed for since the Garden of Eden.

I believe the Antichrist is now alive and preparing to position himself for a phenomenal rise to political power, first in Europe and then globally. I do not know the timing, but I am convinced that it will occur in our lifetime. Daniel 8:23 tells us that the future ruler of the earth will arise "in the latter time of their kingdom" and that "when the transgressors are come to the full, a king of fierce countenance, and understanding dark sentences, shall stand up." The Antichrist will be totally possessed spiritually by Satan, filled with satanic power, and deeply involved with occult power and practices.

The Antichrist's initial political success will cause him to "magnify himself in his heart" and will lead to his blaspheming God (Daniel 8:25). The Antichrist will meet his doom when he battles the armies of heaven at the prophesied Battle of Armageddon and encounters the Lord Jesus Christ and the armies of heaven. Christ will cast him forever into the lake of fire (see Revelation 19:11–21).

PREACHERS OF DECEPTION

I have acquired an extensive library of historical, scientific, political, and prophetic research concerning global government and the world's greatest, most far-reaching, and most devastating pseudoscientific environmental deception. If the forces behind man-made global warming are not stopped, citizens of the West will lose their standard of living and the economic, political, and religious freedoms they value.

The worldview of those who embrace the global-warming theory holds that the existence of the earth, its solar system, and its extremely complex climate system are simply a random accident. They deny divine creation and any plan, purpose, or intention behind the existence of the world. Following that philosophy, leaders of the AGW movement believe they can assume authority to make decisions for the entire human population and for the earth itself. If there is no higher Authority in the universe, as they insist, then they have no Creator or God to answer to. They feel they are free to act in their own political interest, even at the expense of the rest of humanity.

Due to the effectiveness of their propaganda campaign and their skill at manipulating political, educational, and media leaders, the world's population has embraced an astonishingly misguided, extreme "green" philosophy. At the forefront of that philosophy is the demand that humanity dramatically reduce carbon dioxide (CO_2) emissions. The false theory that is presented as an incontrovertible fact is that burning fossil fuels (coal, oil, natural gas) to produce energy is the primary cause of global warming. The rapid warming of the earth's atmosphere, according to AGW theory, will devastate the earth's climate and, ultimately, human life and other species during the next century. The unfounded climate theory, preached as scientific orthodoxy, is built on deliberate deceptions regarding historical falsified temperature records and an unproven scientific climate hypothesis.

The global-government elite, working without legal or constitutional sanction, push the global-warming agenda as the means to achieve their real political goal: establishing a one-world government. The AGW campaign involves requiring by law and international treaty immediate massive reductions in humanity's use of essential fossil fuels, regardless of the massive damage to a nation's economy, industrial production, agriculture, military readiness, and standard of living.

If the citizens of the West fail to challenge the global-warming deception, we can expect to lose the precious liberty our forefathers fought to preserve. In light of the threat posed by AGW alarmists to our freedoms, there are several vital questions that every one of us must seriously consider.

- Is the man-made global-warming crisis a genuine environmental crisis or a skillfully presented lie?
- Is AGW a scientifically proven fact, or is it nothing more than an environmental opinion or preference that is presented as an established scientific theory?
- Is the global-warming "crisis" a fabricated threat that is used to manipulate governments and individual citizens in order to advance a hidden globalist and socialist economic agenda?
- Will a drastic reduction in CO_2 emissions seriously reduce the average global temperature on earth by the year 2100, as the global-warming alarmists propose?
- Is the true primary motive of the AGW movement the minimization of the rise in global temperatures, or is there a sinister and devastating political and economic goal that is never revealed to the public?

The evidence that you will read in the following chapters will show that the claims of the major global-warming alarmists are built on exaggerations and lies. The claims are not supported by independent, verified scientific analysis. The "settled science" of climate change is in reality nothing more authoritative than oft-repeated, loudly proclaimed, high-pressure environmentalist propaganda. The goal of the loudest voices in the movement—including the United Nations Intergovernmental Panel on Climate Change (IPCC) and Al Gore's film *An Inconvenient Truth*—is to frighten citizens, scientists, politicians, and the news media to support an unprecedented growth in global government. An AGW subplot (again, never openly revealed) is to gain socialist-Marxist control of the industries and economies of every nation on earth.

BE PREPARED TO DEFEND YOUR LIBERTIES

Again and again, the message of the Scriptures is to be prepared, and much of being prepared involves becoming aware of the dangers. If the Western nations submit to the demands of the AGW movement, it will result in several disasters. The AGW plans to drastically limit man-made global warming will inevitably have the following consequences:

- the destruction of tens of millions of jobs in the United States
- the transfer from the West of hundreds of billions of dollars in economic production annually, which will be sent to the Third World, including China and India as well as Africa
- seriously reduced or reversed economic growth in both the developed nations and the Third World
- a dramatically reduced standard of living for most Americans
- destruction of our political and personal freedoms by creating intrusive new political powers and regulations that will control every citizen's private, financial, social, and business life
- drastically reduced production of essential fertilizers and other petroleum-based agrichemicals, resulting in decreased food production. This will have devastating ramifications for feeding the rapidly growing populations of Third World nations, since Western democracies supply most of the essential petroleum-based fertilizers and food exports that are vitally needed in the developing world.

Proposed and existing global-warming legislation, such as the Kyoto Protocol, working in combination with new carbon taxes, higher costs for living and doing business, and new cap-and-trade energy regulations, will have a devastating impact on the prosperity of Western democracies. Increased energy costs alone, caused by new anti-global-warming regulations, will seriously limit economic growth. At the same time, expensive renewable energy, such as wind and solar, will handicap billions of Third World citizens who are working desperately to improve their economic situation. Cheap, reliable energy (from fossil fuels) is essential for people to raise their standard of living from subsistence-level living. As the AGW movement consolidates its power, cheap reliable electricity generated from fossil fuels will become scarce and much more expensive.

THE GLOBAL POLITICS OF GLOBAL WARMING

During his first press conference as incoming European Council president, Herman Van Rompuy hailed 2009 as "the first year of global governance," a reference to the globalist G20 (Group of Twenty, an association of established and developing nations) agenda. He went on to describe the Copenhagen climate summit, a major international initiative orchestrated by AGW alarmists, as "another step towards the global management of our planet."[1]

Mike Thompson, chief meteorologist at Kansas City's WDAF television, sent an e-mail to the *Kansas City Star* stating that the global-warming movement "has become completely political—it's not about science at all.… If science were the objective, then we would be seeing an entirely different debate. But there are agendas at play, and it has undermined the credibility of climate science."[2]

Higher energy costs created by unnecessary limits on the use of fossil fuels are just one of the roundabout ways the AGW forces are slowly bringing the Western world—and beyond that, the developing world—to its knees economically. The globalist elite, pursuing their world-government and socialist-Marxist goals, long ago decided to first promote and then hijack the AGW movement. Their ultimate goal is to quietly transform the economies and the balance of political power in the West and around the world.

Havel Wolf, a leading member of the Seattle Audubon Society, strongly supports the AGW position. Wolf declared his real political agenda in 1998, stating that the Communist Party USA's environmental program "presents a viable plan to carry out on the long march to socialism."[3]

According to *A Skeptical Layman's Guide to Man-Made Global Warming*, "In America, socialism is bent on removing individual freedoms and placing the government in charge of our lives. The global warming issue is an important strategy for the advancement of socialism, under the guise of saving the Earth."[4]

Professor Louis Proyect of Columbia University is quoted as saying, "The answer to global warming is in the abolition of private property and production for human need. A socialist world would place an enormous priority on alternative energy sources. This is what ecologically-minded socialists have been exploring for quite some time now."[5]

Maurice F. Strong, a Canadian billionaire, served as conference secretary-general of the pivotal Rio Earth Summit in 1992. The summit attracted the participation of 172 nations and 108 heads of state. Strong, a supporter of global government, has declared, "Current lifestyles and consumption patterns of the affluent middle class—involving high meat intake,...use of fossil fuels, appliances, home and work-place air-conditioning, and suburban housing—are not sustainable. A shift is necessary towards lifestyles less geared to environmentally damaging consumption patterns."[6]

The long-term goal of such environmental ideology is nothing less than the imposition of massive legal, financial, and environmental restrictions on

your government, your business, and your personal lifestyle. AGW supporters want to dictate your diet, your air conditioning, and your driving choices.
Even Nazi Germany and Soviet Russia did not micromanage the lifestyles of
individual citizens to this intrusive degree.

Internet and journal articles about global warming and socialism often
quote Al Gore: "We must take bold and unequivocal action: we must make
the rescue of the environment *the central organizing principle* for civilization."[7]
Gore's goal—and the goal of many of those who are promoting the man-
made global-warming agenda—is to utterly transform Western society. This
means moving the West away from Judeo-Christian principles, democracy, a
free-enterprise market economy, and the protection of private-property rights
as fundamental to a free society. The AGW alarmists will not be satisfied
until they have enacted and enforced enormous increases in carbon energy
taxes and massive environmental regulations, much of it linked to limiting
carbon emissions. But limiting carbon emissions is actually a front for achieving the transformation of previously free-enterprise-based, democratic nations
into a new socialist global government.

Having studied the history and political trends that are evident in the
European Union, the world's first transnational superstate, I can assure you
that true democracy and responsive representative government in Europe have
already been transformed into something virtually unrecognizable. Sovereign
nations have been reconstituted into a 500-million-citizen, twenty-seven-
nation monstrous unresponsive bureaucracy. In the European Union, decisions
are now made in secret by an elite twenty-seven-member European Commission. This sovereign, appointed policy-making body is not accountable to voters. Working alone, it chooses and enacts the policies, laws, taxes, regulations,
and executives that control the lives of half a billion citizens of a formerly
democratic Europe. Welcome to a preview of the coming global government.

SOCIALISM AND THE GLOBAL-WARMING INDUSTRY

An enormous number of people work in the climate-change community. This includes climate scientists, academics, financial leaders, media personalities, nongovernmental organizations, politicians, bureaucrats, United Nations officials, investors in "green" industries, and huge multinational corporations. Together, these individuals, groups, institutions, and corporations form the "global-warming industry." Those in the "industry" have committed their careers, finances, and reputations to the support and propagation of the AGW theory. Any serious examination of the writings and speeches of those who lead the global-warming industry reveals an unvarying tendency to promote much greater government intervention in the lives of all citizens.

Leaders of the global-warming complex are motivated by a desire to bankrupt sovereign Western nations. A primary approach already being used is to create a straitjacket of environmental and economic regulations, excessive energy taxes, and laws that drain the economies of nations that support the global-warming agenda. The resulting weakness motivates the leaders and citizens to submit to the global treaties that reduce their national sovereignty and independence.

Remarkably, the Spanish government, one of the strongest European socialist supporters of anticarbon policies, admitted to the economically disabling effects of adhering to AGW policies and requirements. In a secret report leaked in May 2010, Spain acknowledged it was facing an unprecedented economic disaster primarily due to excessive national debt and growing deficits caused by its extreme environmental policies. Spain has been spending enormous amounts of money on promoting inefficient wind power and solar panels, which has added billions of euros annually to the energy costs of Spanish citizens. The cost of all the energy produced in Spain, including wind, solar, and coal, has doubled due to their expensive renewable-energy policies.[8]

Incredibly, the Obama administration and Democratic members of the U.S. Senate followed Spain's pro-renewable energy policies and introduced their anticarbon legislative agenda, which was misleadingly called the American Power Act. For reasons that are obvious, based on the candid admissions of the government of Spain, this proposed legislation should be called the American Power-Grab Act.

Beyond the very effective use of propaganda, the best tools available to the supporters of AGW are laws, regulations, AGW educational programs, and international treaties. We have seen proposals by environmentalists to use laws and environmental regulations not only to influence the marketplace but also to micromanage the lives and personal activities of individual citizens. The AGW supporters would have you believe that government control, a reduced standard of living, and loss of freedom are necessary to save the world. What follows is only a partial list of the proposed environmental regulations. But it is enough to provide a preview of the coming restrictions, laws, and taxes that AGW environmentalists have planned for you and your neighbors.

- ban open fires and wood-burning and coal-burning stoves
- ban incandescent light bulbs
- ban bottled water
- ban private cars from some areas
- ban plasma televisions
- ban new airports and the expansion of existing airports
- ban "standby mode" on appliances (which is what allows remotes to turn them on)
- ban coal-fired electric-power generation
- ban electric hot-water systems
- ban families from vacationing by car

- ban three-day weekends that encourage vacation travel
- tax babies to force people to commit to family planning, resulting in fewer children
- tax large cars that get lower gas mileage
- tax an individual's production of rubbish
- tax second homes
- tax second cars
- tax holiday airline flights
- tax electricity in order to generate revenue to subsidize solar power
- levy an eco-tax on cars entering cities
- require permits to drive your car outside your city
- limit one's choice when buying a new appliance
- issue carbon credits (limits annually) to every person and family
- remove white lines on roads to make motorists drive more carefully[9]

We are fast approaching a major crisis. I anticipate the introduction of measures to reduce agricultural yield and food production in both the West and the Third World. These measures include limitations on fertilizer production and use, higher energy costs, and other restrictions, as well as regulations that will limit agriculture in the biggest food-producing nations. The result will be that the West will be less able to assist in efforts to feed the Third World, radically shifting world opinion against the West and its generally democratic ideology.

EXPOSING THE ULTIMATE GOAL

A far-reaching political conspiracy is well underway to position man-made global warming as the *leading threat* to humanity and the earth's climate. In later chapters we will discuss the deliberate falsification of historic temperature data, the silencing of skeptical climate scientists whose research has disproved AGW, and other pertinent climate data. But for now, it is important to establish that the effort to utilize man-made global warming as a lever to achieve world domination is already far advanced in its implementation.

The history and development of the man-made global-warming conspiracy is relatively easy to document. The Club of Rome, a globalist European think tank, published in 1993 a document titled "The First Global Revolution." This document outlines their plans to use the fabricated environmental crisis of global warming to stampede humanity to achieve the club's hidden goal: global government. The chilling language of the document reveals their deeply cynical plans to impose global government on all citizens of every nation:

> In searching for a common enemy against whom we can unite, *we came up with the idea that pollution, the threat of global warming,* water shortages, famine and the like, *would fit the bill.* In their totality and their interactions these phenomena do constitute a common threat which must be confronted by everyone together.... All these dangers are caused by *human intervention* in natural processes, and it is only through changed attitudes and behavior that they can be overcome. *The real enemy then is humanity itself.*[10]

Please carefully consider the implications of the final sentence: "The real enemy then is humanity itself." Throughout this book you will see evidence of the AGW movement's preference for nonhuman species, including their goal to achieve the massive reduction of the human population of earth.

The deep cynicism and deceit of the global-warming alarmists is confirmed in this statement by Professor Daniel Botkin: "Some colleagues who share some of my doubts [about global warming and its possible causes] argue that the only way to get our society to truly change is to frighten people with the possibility of a catastrophe."[11]

I will demonstrate in chapter 3 that the propaganda claims made by global-warming alarmists are inflated and often patently false. Their initial purpose, by their own admission, was to create a worldwide wave of environmental fear and panic that served to motivate political leaders, the media, and billions of people to support climate-change policies. Those policies will have the effect of diverting hundreds of billions of tax dollars annually out of the economies of Western nations and into ineffective efforts to reduce the Third World's annual production of CO_2.

North Americans and Europeans are familiar with the leading exponent of man-made global warming, Al Gore. Gore wrote in his 1992 pivotal environmental book *Earth in the Balance:* "Adopting a central organizing principle—one agreed to voluntarily—means embarking on an all-out effort to use every policy and program, every law and institution, every treaty and alliance, every tactic and strategy, every plan and course of action—to use in short, every means to halt the destruction of the environment and to preserve and nurture our ecological system."[12] In other words, Gore demands that everyone embrace the cause of saving the planet from man-made global warming as the only effective way to mobilize the public to demand massive economic, political, and social change to save the environment.

American novelist, essayist, and humorist Mark Twain once stated, "Everybody talks about the weather, but nobody does anything about it." Today, a global environmental movement claims that it is trying to change the global climate, but in reality it is pursuing a very different goal and a hidden political agenda.

The man-made global-warming alarmist campaign is intended to produce a powerful world-governmental body under the authority of the United Nations. This new global regime will constitute a socialist-Marxist environmental dictatorship that will possess total legal authority to control the lives and actions of every citizen, every corporation, and every nation on earth. It will gain political control by using the illusion that unquestioned environmental regulation is essential to save humanity from an imminent global-warming catastrophe. The reality, however, is that the global-warming deception is the greatest fraud in the history of science.

Professor Harold Lewis, one of the most respected and published physicists in the world, is emeritus professor of physics at the University of California, Santa Barbara. After sixty-seven years of membership, in October 2010, Dr. Lewis sent his letter of resignation to the American Physical Society (one of the United States' most prestigious scientific organizations) addressed to its president, Curtis G. Callan Jr, at Princeton University. Dr. Lewis wrote: "[Global warming] is the greatest and most successful pseudoscientific fraud I have seen in my long life."[13]

The evidence in the following chapters will document that this global-warming campaign has little to do with saving the earth. *National Post* commentator Peter Foster wrote about the true motives of AGW alarmists: "Leftists are inclined to believe in climate change because its 'solutions'—central control and wealth redistribution—are things they already desire."[14]

Dr. Kiminori Itoh, a Japanese member of the IPCC as well as an award-winning environmental physical chemist and scientist, warned about the ultimate fallout when the general public becomes aware of the gigantic hoax of man-made global-warming alarmism: "Warming fears are the 'worst scientific scandal' in…history…. When people come to know what the truth is, they will feel deceived by science and scientists."[15]

THE CHRISTIAN'S PERSPECTIVE

Every new piece of evidence of the fulfillment of end-times prophecy in our generation alerts us to the soon return of Jesus Christ. We are also assured by the Bible that humanity does not possess the power to destroy the earth—either gradually through climate change or through sudden cataclysm, such as nuclear holocaust. God and only God holds the power to alter the earth, and the earth's future remains securely in His hands. As the Scriptures declare, "One generation passeth away, and another generation cometh: but the earth abideth forever" (Ecclesiastes 1:4). The destiny of the earth and humanity remains solely in God's command.

Globalists are using scare tactics to promote a counterfeit environmental crisis. They make liberal use of media deception as well as falsified historical temperature data and spurious climate research. They espouse their theories, calling them factual and science based, while in truth they are based on a massive deception. The globalists have reframed the research data and, in some cases, silenced scientists whose research contradicts their AGW propaganda. They trumpet their own skewed computer-model scenarios in an effort to push representatives of sovereign nations toward world government, fueled by humanity's unwarranted fear of a coming climate disaster.

While the globalists use fear of man-made global warming as a tactic and methodology, Christians know that the holy love of our all-powerful God banishes all fear: "There is no fear in love; but perfect love casteth out fear: because fear hath torment. He that feareth is not made perfect in love" (1 John 4:18). Truth will guide us and reassure us as we learn the truth about the AGW deception, and as we decide how to expose the AGW deception and stand for God and His truth in the world.

The Pervasive Myth of Man-Made Global Warming

Humanity faces an unprecedented enemy bent on controlling our lives and destroying virtually everything we value most—our social, economic, and political freedoms; our autonomy and opportunities; even our freedom to make our own choices and personal decisions. Everything we cherish is facing the greatest threat since the darkest days of World War II. In the early 1940s, it seemed that Nazi Germany, Italy, and Japan might defeat the combined military forces of the United States, England, Russia, Canada, and the other Allies. Hitler's unspeakably evil vision of world domination would have become a devastating reality if the Axis powers had prevailed. A defeat of the Allies would have installed an evil totalitarian regime that would have enslaved every person on earth. All hope would have been extinguished for those who cherish liberty and freedom.

Today a similar lust for global political, economic, and spiritual domination has taken hold in the centers of political power around the world. These globalist forces seek absolute control as they reach into military, economic, social, political, and even religious institutions. And unlike Adolf Hitler, who built a formidable military force that invaded and occupied sovereign nations, the new global threat is cloaked in a deceptive environmental cause that promises false benefits to all of humanity. Today's globalists cloak their totalitarian agenda in the seemingly laudable cause of saving the world from rising global temperatures resulting from the use of fossil fuels to produce energy. They are so skilled in public relations and sophisticated propaganda that most of us are blind to the evil that is hidden behind the public face of the anthropogenic global warming (AGW) movement.

If human-caused global warming were a scientific fact, and if massive changes in energy policy could actually reverse the trend, it would be a worthy cause. But the only global warming that can be verified by unbiased scientific research is minimal, at 1°F since 1900. That slight increase was caused not by rising levels of man-made carbon dioxide (CO_2) emissions, but primarily by natural variations in solar radiation, cloud coverage, and volcanic eruptions. The biggest danger facing humanity is not from carbon dioxide emissions but rather from AGW's massive campaign of lies and the subsequent edicts and international treaties that abrogate the constitutions of sovereign nations, the rights of corporations, and the freedoms of individual citizens throughout the world.

The theory that global warming is caused primarily by the burning of fossil fuels is presented by the United Nations and the global media as an unquestioned scientific fact. Hence, the propaganda campaign demands that all people of good will join the AGW cause and oppose the continued use of fossil fuels to produce energy. This, and only this, will assure the survival of humanity, according to supporters of the AGW movement.

In truth, the anti-global-warming initiative has almost nothing to do with saving humanity from rising temperatures. The reality is that it has everything to do with the coming subjugation of democratic nations, institutions, and individuals to the dictatorial requirements of the AGW elite. Global warming has been chosen as the cause célèbre. The real hidden agenda is to take control of the political, economic, financial, and military institutions of every nation on earth.

THE FRAUDULENT THEORY OF GLOBAL WARMING

History shows that fear is an effective motivator of people, especially on a mass scale. Knowing that a frontal attack would have little chance of succeeding, the globalist elite has seized on international concern over global warming. Citizens of Western democracies would not knowingly yield to a socialist globalist elite that showed its true plans to eradicate our democratic freedoms. But by emphasizing the dangers of melting icecaps, expanding deserts, and dramatic shifts in weather patterns, the globalists have found it easy to generate massive political, educational, and media support. Who wants to see the coastal areas flooded, agricultural production decimated, population centers threatened with rising sea levels, and arable land turned to desert? The socialist-globalists have found a vital environmental issue that elicits exactly the emotional and political reaction they are looking for.

Globalists now have a tool they can use to gradually impose their socialistic-Marxist environmental regulatory control around the world. If the AGW strategy is not exposed and opposed by Western democracies, we will lose our vital political, economic, and religious freedom. It is time to awaken to the growing danger and alert our elected representatives in government.

You might be wondering: *Why would a political elite choose to employ an unrelated environmental issue to use as leverage in achieving a centralized global government? Why not promote a widely accepted political cause such as eliminating hunger or poverty or disease?* Those are valid questions, and they reveal the intelligent deviousness of the globalist strategy.

Hunger does not affect everyone, and especially in the developed and industrialized world, it is an issue that can be held at arm's length. Likewise with poverty or housing or economic opportunity. These are pressing issues in the Third World, but for most citizens in the industrialized nations these issues can easily be ignored and overlooked by most citizens.

Not so with global warming. If the earth's temperature steadily increases due to continuing human production of CO_2, then no one will be immune to the disastrous consequences. East or West, wealthy or poor, industrialized or agrarian, every human will be affected negatively. That is what makes the man-made global-warming cause so effective and so difficult to oppose. It allows globalist leaders to present themselves as the good guys, the saviors of the environment, and by extension, the rescuers of humanity.

THE PERFECT TIMING FOR A GLOBALIST OFFENSIVE

There is a second major reason that exploiting the global-warming deception is such an effective political strategy. And that reason has to do with timing. The AGW movement gained momentum following the failure of socialism and Communism in Russia, Eastern Europe, and China to deliver economic success and social justice. With the power centers of Communism either disbanded or now relying on a type of modified capitalism for economic growth (as in China), the globalist elite was initially left at a severe disadvantage. However, they have not abandoned the goal of achieving absolute control over every nation on earth. Because socialism has been shown to be impotent as an economic and social control system, globalists had to recalibrate and change their approach.

The cause of global warming presented itself as a universal concern, so globalists started promoting the threat as the pervasive "enemy of the people." Globalists positioned themselves as the only viable force that could marshal scientists, policy makers, government leaders, and others with the necessary knowledge, authority, and expertise to overcome the threat to the environment. If life on earth was to be spared, then the environmental globalists would have to be taken seriously. Eventually, leaders in the anthropogenic global-warming movement found allies within the United Nations, who led the attack against the growing use of fossil fuels. They made use of international climate-change summits (in Kyoto and Copenhagen) to pressure national governments into agreeing to limits on fossil fuels. The resulting UN-mandated environmental agreements imposed staggering reductions in man-made CO_2 emissions from the use of fossil fuels to generate electricity as well as transportation and industry.

Václav Klaus was the president of the Czech Republic and a noted economist. In his book *Blue Planet in Green Shackles,* he warns that the global-warming movement has been hijacked by socialist-Communists. Klaus, who endured thirty years of Communist rule in Eastern Europe, wrote, *"Green is the new red....* Today's debate about global warming is essentially a debate about freedom. The environmentalists would like to mastermind each and every possible (and impossible) aspect of our lives.... The suppression of contrary ideas is probably more dangerous to society than global warming."[1]

He added, "The theory of global warming and the hypothesis on its causes, which has spread around massively nowadays, may be a bad theory, it may also be a valueless theory, but in any case it is a very dangerous theory."[2]

Once a lie is established in the minds of a majority of citizens, even a highly debatable myth can take on a life of its own. The myth is gradually accepted as self-evident truth, and it alters the behavior, attitudes, and expectations of millions of citizens. Political commentator H. L. Mencken was the most prominent American newspaperman and book reviewer of the 1920s. He was a shrewd judge of the motives and plans of the politicians he interviewed and wrote about. He warned that "civilization, in fact, grows more and more maudlin and hysterical; especially under democracy it tends to degenerate into a mere combat of crazes; the whole aim of practical politics is to keep the populace alarmed (and hence clamorous to be led to safety) by an endless series of hobgoblins, most of them imaginary."[3]

This is one of the reasons it's important for everyone, Christians especially, to look at the facts behind the myths about climate change. Throughout history, the earth has been subject to marked changes in the climate. Over epochs, the temperature rises and drops. Sea levels rise and fall. Ice sheets and glaciers expand and retreat. Species become extinct. The earth that God created and gave humanity dominion over is a dynamic and constantly changing planet. The geological history of the earth reveals that the planet has always been in a state of climate change. Global warming is occurring in our generation, but only very gradually and almost entirely due to natural factors. Humanity's use of fossil fuels and the rising level of CO_2 in the atmosphere have relatively little to do with it. (We will explore the evidence regarding the real impacts on global warming and climate change in chapter 8.)

A SUMMARY OF GLOBAL TEMPERATURE HISTORY

The earth does not maintain a static climate. Our planet's climate is constantly changing as it is subjected to influences from a variety of natural phenomena, including solar radiation, the effect of the moon's gravitational pull, massive amounts of the sun's cosmic rays and extraterrestrial dust, tectonic plate movements, the effects of the Gulf Stream on weather patterns, and emissions of carbon dioxide from volcanic eruptions.

The Roman Warm Period—from 250 BC to AD 450

European and North African populations living near the Mediterranean Sea enjoyed an unusually warm period for seven centuries, from 250 BC until approximately AD 450. Very little ice or snow was recorded in the Roman records during that period. Average temperatures increased by 2°C to 6°C (3.6°F to 10.8°F). This prolonged warm period led to widespread prosperity and high agricultural production throughout the Roman Empire.

The Dark Ages Cold Period—from AD 535 to AD 900

Geologic evidence reveals that there was a prolonged cooling period known as the Dark Ages Cold Period that continued from approximately AD 535 until AD 900. During this cooling period, European civilization declined—with poor agricultural production, poor health, and a general retreat from the previous advances in civilization.

The Medieval Warm Period—AD 900 to AD 1300

The centuries from 900 to 1300 (known as the Medieval Warm Period) witnessed a significant warming period. Average temperatures registered slightly more than 2°F higher than the earth's current climate. This rise in global temperature resulted in tremendous benefits for the Western world and the Northern Hemisphere. As just one early example: Vikings conquered Greenland and started growing grapevines in previously uninhabitable areas. They produced crops for food and fermented grapes for wine in a region that previously was far from arable.

The Medieval Warm Period, although well documented by historians and climate scientists, has been deliberately minimized by the climate scientists who embrace the theory of man-made global warming. The Medieval Warm Period's increase in global temperatures of 2°F was unrelated to any increase in carbon dioxide emissions due to human activity. At that time there were low population levels and no industrialization, and thus virtually no significant human contribution to increased CO_2 levels. The warming period that followed AD 900 had nothing to do with human activity. And instead of leading to a climate disaster, the four centuries of the Medieval Warm Period led to enhanced growing seasons, increased crop (and thus food) production, and a significant rise in European prosperity.

The Little Ice Age—AD 1350 to AD 1850

As one would expect, historical records indicate that climate conditions continued to change. From 1350 until 1850, the world experienced what is called the Little Ice Age. Global temperature dropped significantly when the climate of northern Europe cooled for almost five hundred years—with temperatures falling almost 3°F. For five centuries following AD 1350, colder temperatures produced massive economic, social, and health-related hardships for the populations of northern Europe and North America. And again, since this period predates the rapid expansion of the Industrial Revolution and the acceleration of technology, there is no correlation between climate change and rising levels of CO_2 in the atmosphere.

ADAPTING TO CHANGE

A quick look at the history of climate change shows that global warming is not a recent phenomenon. But that does not prevent the false preachers of man-made global warming from shouting their alarmist theories as if we are now experiencing an unprecedented change in the earth's temperature. We should not fear a change in the earth's climate. Instead, we need to use our intelligence and creativity to adapt to a naturally changing environment.

Professor William Soon, a Harvard University astrophysicist and geophysicist, has said he is "embarrassed and puzzled"[4] by the shallow science that is revealed in numerous papers that support the proposition that the earth faces an overwhelming climate crisis caused by global warming. And while climate-change alarmists profess extreme fear about the continued rise of man-made carbon dioxide in the atmosphere, the current concentration of CO_2 at around 385 parts per million by volume (ppmv) is historically quite low. We live in a somewhat carbon-deficient atmosphere compared to the amount of CO_2 that existed in the atmosphere during most of earth's history.

Scientists have been measuring atmospheric CO_2 levels for two centuries now. From 1812 until 1961, climate scientists used the Pettenkofer method (a chemical method) to measure CO_2 levels with an accuracy of 1 to 3 percent. In the century and a half ending in 1961, the scientists measured the CO_2 levels in the air 90,000 times. During that time carbon dioxide levels in the atmosphere were higher than today's CO_2 level of 385 ppmv (parts per million by volume) in 1825, 1857, and 1942. For example, in 1942 the Pettenkofer method registered 400 ppmv which is [about 4 percent] higher than today's level of 385 ppmv.[5]

Higher levels of atmospheric CO_2 in history were not caused by man-made carbon dioxide emissions. Likewise, temperature fluctuations and historic levels of carbon dioxide do not establish a cause-and-effect linkage between CO_2 levels and increased average global temperatures.

In 1959 climate scientists shifted exclusively to a new CO_2 measurement technique using infrared spectroscopy. In the last half century they have used this method at the Mauna Loa atmospheric measuring station atop this Hawaiian volcano. Unfortunately, the infrared spectroscopy method has not been tested against the older Pettenkofer method, so we cannot be certain if the two methods are comparable and equally accurate.[6]

William Kininmonth, a former head of the National Climate Center and a consultant to the World Meteorological Organization, wrote that "the likely extent of global temperature rise from a doubling of CO_2 is less than 1[°]C. Such warming is well within the envelope of [climate] variation experienced during the past 10,000 years and insignificant in the context of glacial cycles during the past million years, when Earth has been predominantly very cold and covered by extensive ice sheets."[7]

Humans are an incredibly adaptive species who have learned to survive and prosper in environments as diverse as subzero conditions (even −30°F) at the North Pole and the extreme heat of 120°F in the Kalahari Desert. The naive assumption made by global-warming alarmists is that neither humanity nor the thousands of animal species would be able to adapt and prosper on a warmer planet. Their position is contradicted by human experience throughout history and ample scientific evidence of animals' adaptations to changes in climate. If species could not adapt and move when confronted with climate changes, they would have become extinct.

God created and controls the universe, and only He understands fully the complex processes that take place in the world He created. God also created humanity and gave man the intelligence, resourcefulness, and adaptability to thrive on the earth in radically different climates. The globalists employ fear as a propaganda tool, but Christians know that God is the true Lord of creation, and thus we have no reason to be distracted or intimidated by the AGW lies.

HUMANITY'S EFFECT ON ATMOSPHERIC CHANGE

In any honest discussion of global warming, we need to place humanity's annual production of carbon dioxide in perspective. In reality, CO_2 comprises only a tiny component of the earth's atmosphere, just 0.038 percent. *That is only thirty-eight parts in one-thousandth of 1 percent* of the earth's atmosphere. Humanity contributes only 3 percent of the annual global emissions of CO_2. The combined quantities of CO_2 stored in the depths of the oceans, the soil, and in the limestone of the earth's crust dwarf the tiny amounts of CO_2 that humans produce through the use of fossil fuels.

The AGW movement makes much of "greenhouse gases," arguing that they must be reduced if we are to survive on earth. However, carbon dioxide makes up only 3 percent of all greenhouse gases. Some 95 percent of greenhouse gases are composed of invisible water vapor (not that portion visible in clouds), and water vapor is something that humanity cannot possibly reduce. Water vapor is far and away the most significant gas that affects global temperature.

During the last century and a half, the Industrial Revolution greatly expanded and accelerated the use of fossil fuels in manufacturing and for generating electricity. In the twentieth century, petroleum use increased greatly as fuel for various forms of transportation—from diesel locomotives to trucks, cars, buses, and aircraft. In the last century and a half, the average global surface temperature rose by less than 1°C (only 0.7°C, or 1.3°F).[8] However, since 1998, the earth has been gradually cooling, losing most of the temperature gains from earlier in the century.[9]

HOW GLOBAL WARMING IS DEFINED

Generally, global warming is defined as the measured continual increase in the average global temperature of the earth's surface air and oceans since approximately 1860 and its continued projection to the year 2100. The 2007 United Nations Intergovernmental Panel on Climate Change (IPCC) report declared that the global surface temperature has increased 0.74 ± 0.18°C (1.33 ± 0.32°F) between 1900 and 2000. In other words, the IPCC concluded that global temperatures increased three-quarters of 1°C (plus or minus 0.18°C).[10] This translates into a rise of approximately 1.3°F in the last century, but with an error factor of 0.32°F. So scientific records declare that global temperature has definitely risen 1°F (1.3 minus 0.32) from 1900 till 2000.

Those who support the global-warming alarmist position believe that most of the temperature increase since the 1860s was caused by increased levels of greenhouse gases, especially CO_2, from approximately 250 ppmv in 1860 to 385 ppmv in 2010. The man-made global-warming theory suggests that the rise in CO_2 results primarily, if not solely, from human activity. The theory also assumes that the observed rise in global temperature during the last century was caused by the rise in the level of CO_2 in the atmosphere.

The 2007 IPCC report's main conclusion declared that the measured increase in global temperature during the last five decades "was 'very likely' due to" increasing levels of atmospheric CO_2, produced primarily by the burning of fossil fuels and other human activities, such as deforestation.[11]

However, there are other natural processes on earth and in space—including solar cycles and cloud formation developments—that can elevate global temperatures, quite apart from the levels of CO_2 in the atmosphere. Roy W. Spencer, a climatologist and author of the book *Climate Confusion,* wrote, "A minority of climate researchers have maintained that some—or even most—of [the last fifty years of] warming could have been due to natural causes. For instance, the Pacific Decadal Oscillation (PDO) and Atlantic Multi-decadal Oscillation (AMO) are natural modes of climate variability which have similar time scales to warming and cooling periods during the 20th Century."[12]

The PDO referred to by Spencer is a Pacific climate variability pattern that impacts temperature cycles over twenty to thirty years in the Pacific Ocean above a latitude of 20°N. The PDO causes either warmer or cooler surface waters in the northern Pacific Ocean, depending on the cycle. The AMO is a variability cycle that occurs in the North Atlantic Ocean which also can affect the sea's surface temperature. The El Niño–Southern Oscillation (ENSO) is a major, five-year-long climate cycle in the tropical Pacific Ocean, but it can vary from three to seven years. In Spanish, *El Niño* means "the boy" and is a reference to the Christ child because it usually occurs during the Christmas season. El Niño is often associated with weather disturbances that can lead to floods and droughts.

The global-warming propagandists studiously ignore the effects of natural phenomena. Further, supporters of AGW completely overlook the fact that historically, humanity generally has prospered during periods in which the average temperature rose several degrees. However, historical evidence shows that periods of significantly colder climate (the Little Ice Age, for example) were characterized by significant loss of population, severe societal disruption, wars, disease (including plague), species extinctions, drought, and famine.

The news media tend to magnify the deaths of vulnerable population groups (the very young and the elderly) who succumb to heat waves, such as the one in Europe that contributed to as many as two hundred thousand deaths in 2003. However, the much colder temperatures that occur during European winters cause approximately 1.5 million deaths every year.[13] Thus, cold temperatures were responsible for seven and a half times more deaths than occurred in 2003 during an excessive heat wave. Unfortunately, the media doesn't consider the cold-weather deaths of millions of primarily older EU citizens to be newsworthy.

In the next chapter we will examine the pervasive propaganda campaign that has convinced millions of people that "man-made" global warming poses a grave threat to our future. This alarmist campaign is pushing the idea that we must submit to massive carbon taxes and a severe reduction in our standard of living to save the planet.

The Propaganda Campaign That Advances Global Government

O ne of the most effective strategies to gain support for the sinister globalist agenda is to link it to something that is urgent and beneficial. Efforts that promise to save the environment attract constant media attention, which leaves the globalist promoters free to work behind the scenes to advance their hidden political agenda.

Long ago, globalists realized they could mobilize enormous numbers of people by enlisting them in the "green" cause of protecting humanity against anthropogenic global warming (AGW). Most people will get behind a cause when they believe their children's and grandchildren's survival depends on their actions today. In making the reduction of carbon dioxide emissions to combat global warming the centerpiece of their propaganda campaign, globalists are advancing their true cause without attracting attention to it.

John Bellamy Foster was editor of the Marxist magazine *Monthly Review*. In 2005, he acknowledged that a gradualist approach was the Communists' only hope for converting Americans first to socialism and, eventually, to Communism. As much as Foster hates socialism, which he considers the "weak sister" of Communism, he recognized that America would never knowingly accept Communism. However, U.S. citizens could be induced to accept socialism if they didn't realize what was actually occurring. If they could be convinced to accept socialist principles and practices, but under a different name, it would place America on a political path that would lead inevitably to the Communist hell that was being prepared for it. Foster admitted, "The problem is capitalism. The only solution, as difficult as this may be to contemplate at the present time, is socialism."[1]

As a dedicated Communist, Foster was unhappy that they could not immediately impose a Communist dictatorship on the United States but would have to settle for establishing socialism first. He realized that the global-warming campaign could be used to create overly intrusive laws and restrictive environmental regulations that would eventually lead to the outcome that he desired.

SOCIALISM AND THE PUSH FOR GLOBALISM

Socialist-Marxist ideology motivates international political efforts to combat so-called AGW. Global warming serves as a convenient—and very effective—cause to acclimate citizens to socialist policies. These include laws, environmental regulations, and international climate-control treaties designed to eventually abolish the right to own and control private property.

From the first introduction of Marxist and socialist political philosophy in the mid-1800s, those who embrace this satanic philosophy have expressed hatred for private ownership of property. They disdain the libertarian principles that laid the foundation of the American and Canadian dream of limited, constitutional, representative government.

The founders of the United States cherished the concept of "a government of laws; not of men." In 1780, John Adams included this vital principle in the Massachusetts constitution to reflect the political concept that Americans were to be governed by laws that applied to all people equally, rather than being ruled by the arbitrary dictates of aristocrats and government officials.

The founders created a unique political system that would protect citizens against arbitrary excesses of judicial and legislative power. As stated in the Declaration of Independence, they sought to limit the possibility of a future government seizing control of the inalienable [God-given] rights of liberty, freedom, and the pursuit of happiness. The term *inalienable* means these rights are not arbitrarily granted by the government of the day, but that all citizens are "endowed" with these rights "by their Creator." Because these fundamental rights are given by God, they can't be repudiated by any government now or in the future. This radical concept established, for the first time in history, the principle that there were definite limits on a government's powers and the laws it could impose on citizens. This fundamental governing principle limited the government, then and in the future, from imposing arbitrary laws.

Today, however, we commonly encounter politicians, judges, and bureaucrats who no longer believe in God or in the supreme legal authority of the U.S. Constitution. They trample on the fundamental principles that form the basis of the American dream. They willingly violate the vision of the nation's founders and the clear intent of the U.S. Constitution, which strictly limited the federal government's control over the lives of citizens. As a result of more than six decades of liberal influence in public education, American students are inundated with anticonservative, antibusiness, and antireligious attitudes.

Teachers no longer embrace the dream of limited constitutional government but usually see themselves as agents of change. An example of this approach is found in *Educational Leadership,* March 1993 issue, in the article "Why Teachers Must Become Change Agents" by Michael G. Fullan.

Many work to mold the next generation of American youth to accept a socialist view of government and the economy.[2]

Karl Marx and Friedrich Engels wrote their major work, *The Communist Manifesto,* in 1848. Their atheistic philosophy gave birth to the godless socialist-Communist political movement that destroyed numerous nations and economies, as well as the lives of more than 100 million people. Those who resisted the Communists' attacks on religious and political freedom and free enterprise were imprisoned or executed. Marx wrote, "The theory of Communism can be summed up in a single sentence: Abolition of private property."[3]

To advance the cause of Marxism, followers of Communism attack a God-given, inalienable right: that of private ownership of property. The right to possess, use, buy, sell, and transfer property is a fundamental human right, without which all other liberties become virtually meaningless. Private-property rights acknowledge that we have a right to enjoy the benefits that accrue from our labor and our possessions. When private-property rights are limited or virtually eliminated by laws, actions, and policies of government, then citizens can no longer enjoy the fruits of their work. Instead, we end up working primarily to pay taxes to support government redistribution programs.

Excessive taxation is but one of the evidences of efforts worldwide to transfer the wealth, property, and power from individual citizens to a centralized government. Communists and socialists know that the vast majority of Americans love their liberty as well as the rights and protections granted by the Constitution. It is known that most Americans embrace the concept of limited representative government. Citizens would never knowingly accept a socialist-Marxist political system, that same system that has imprisoned political opponents, done away with free speech, imposed a one-party system, waged genocide campaigns, created massive famines, and destroyed the economies and the ecology of Russia, China, North Korea, Cuba, much of Eastern Europe, and many other parts of the world. Further, the environmental record of the Communists ruling Russia, China, Ethiopia, North Korea, and Cuba is absolutely appalling.

In light of the clear and condemning historical record, Communists and socialists chose to disguise their goals to achieve a socialist global government. The available and very effective disguise is to position their movement as an international "save the earth" effort. And the biggest enemy of the environment, in their propaganda scenario, is greedy, uncaring Western capitalism. As long ago as 1972, Gus Hall, then national chairman of the Communist Party USA, declared, "Human society cannot basically stop the destruction of the environment under capitalism. Socialism is the only structure that makes it possible."[4] However, the ruling Communist regimes in Russia, China, and North Korea have produced staggering levels of environmental destruction and wholesale disaster. Another statement that reveals the socialist agenda behind the AGW campaign comes from Professor Maurice King: "Global Sustainability requires the deliberate quest of poverty, reduced resource consumption and set levels of mortality control."[5]

Spelling out with some specifics exactly how socialists intend to eliminate the freedoms we enjoy, Canadian billionaire Maurice Strong clarified the socialist goals at the 1992 Rio Earth Summit. "Current lifestyles and consumption patterns of the affluent middle class—involving high meat intake, use of fossil fuels, appliances, air-conditioning, and suburban housing—are not sustainable."[6]

Carroll Quigley, an American historian, stated in his insightful book *Tragedy and Hope* that the real political and economic control of the major nations during the last century was secretly held by a hidden group of international financial leaders and private bankers.

> In addition to these pragmatic goals, the powers of financial capitalism had another far-reaching aim, nothing less than to create a world system of financial control in private hands able to dominate the political system of each country and the economy of the world as a whole. This system was to be controlled in a feudalist fashion by the central banks of the world acting in concert, by secret agreements arrived at in frequent private meetings and conferences. The apex of the system was to be the Bank for International Settlements in Basle, Switzerland, a private bank owned and controlled by the world's central banks which were themselves private corporations.[7]

CONVENIENT TIMING FOR A NEW PROPAGANDA OFFENSIVE

The Communist Party in Russia and Eastern Europe fell in the late 1980s and early 1990s, after seventy years of brutal control over and destruction of the lives of hundreds of millions of people, first in Russia, then spreading to Eastern Europe after World War II. The left-wing political and philosophical supporters of Marxism and socialism in the West were left adrift. Socialists and Marxists in the West had lost their political inspiration and realized that their academic friends were now contemptuous of their appeals to failed socialist doctrine. Both Communism and its political sister, socialism, had been discredited. Even the Chinese government, after recognizing the bankruptcy of Communist economic theory, adopted Western capitalistic principles of a somewhat free business market—yet still existing under totalitarian political control.

In the West, socialist and Communist political and academic leaders needed to find a new way to repackage and reinvent themselves politically. Most Westerners had no desire to listen to political claims regarding the past glories of socialism in light of its utter economic failure and its suppression of personal freedoms (and massive slaughter of millions of political opponents).

For a few years, some of the newly adrift socialists preached vainly against the increasing free-market globalization of the world's economy. The European antiglobalization movement became the new political home for socialists and Marxists who wanted to reject the rapid growth of capitalism, free markets, and privately owned business. However, antiglobalization never gained much popular appeal or political traction outside France. The massive growth of the worldwide economy provided overwhelming evidence of the benefits of a globally integrated, free-market economy.

Then came the AGW movement, to combat a supposed man-made threat to the survival of the human race. In the early 1990s, the simmering socialist environmental issue moved from the shadows to the front pages of major newspapers. The topic of "man-made warming" often led the way in television talk shows and late-night newscasts. It received an unprecedented boost and unheard-of visibility courtesy of former U.S. Vice President Al Gore. A former U.S. senator, Gore reinvented himself as the leading authority on and spokesman for AGW. He has stated, "The warnings about global warming have been extremely clear for a long time. We are facing a global climate crisis. It is deepening. We are entering a period of consequences."[8]

AGW was found to be the ideal cover story for the socialists' and globalists' underlying political agenda. By pushing AGW, they could simultaneously support extreme socialistic regulatory control of government, business, and individuals while advancing their goal of global government.

The political cover afforded by the AGW cause helped unite disparate political interests. It allowed socialists in the West to gain popular support by fighting against an apparent global economic threat. The left-wing political interests that chose to unite under the AGW banner included socialists, Communists, academic Marxists, progressives, anticapitalists, opponents of global free trade, large corporations, and oil companies. It is worthwhile to note that large corporations and oil companies have found ways to profit from the coming carbon dioxide taxes, cap-and-trade policies, and other environmental regulations.

HOW AGW POLICIES WILL REDUCE OUR STANDARD OF LIVING

Even scientists who support climate-change policies admit that Kyoto Protocol measures designed to reduce the earth's average projected temperature by 2100 will create an *almost undetectable* reduction of only 0.33°F. After ninety years and $16 trillion in environmental subsidies paid to Third World dictators, scientists calculate the effect will be a rise in global temperature of 9.7°F. In the *absence* of enforced restrictions and carbon taxes, the estimated rise in global temperature would be 10°F. Even if the AGW movement was correct, the anticipated reduction of just one-third of 1°F after ninety years of massive sacrifice will come at a tremendous cost: a drop in North America's standard of living to the level of the Great Depression!

What will a ridiculously low reduction in global temperature cost humanity? The cost of the Kyoto Protocol to control man-made global warming will be nearly a century of enormous economic deprivation, as well as the massive reduction of the standard of living and personal freedoms of all citizens in industrialized nations. (This will be fully documented in chapter 9.)

International efforts to reduce the supposed threats of AGW will destroy your political and personal freedom by creating massive new political and regulatory powers over your private, social, and business life. Environmentalist-socialist-globalist groups will have political control of the economy, the lifestyles of all citizens, and the creation of the coming global government as prophesied in the Bible. So what will humanity really gain from the imposition of global-warming policies designed to save us from the exaggerated fears of massive climate change? For an answer, let's look to Maurice Strong, a billionaire and the first executive who directed the UN Environment Program. Strong revealed his contempt for the current lifestyles of North Americans and the free-enterprise business philosophy that created the Western world's prosperity. He declared, "Isn't the only hope for the planet that the industrialized civilizations collapse? Isn't it our responsibility to bring that about?"[9]

Peter Foster, writing for Canada's *National Post,* exposed the growing left-wing political bias evident in the majority of chemical scientists and biologists in North America. "Most people would not be surprised if told there was a leftist bias in political science or English faculties," Foster wrote, "but a 2005 study by academics Stanley Rothman, S. Robert Lichter, and Neil Nevitte found that 'three out of four biologists and computer scientists now place themselves to the left of center, as do about two thirds of mathematicians, chemists, and physicists.' Indeed, among physicists, the study found that self-described Democrats outnumbered Republicans in American universities by more than ten to one!"[10]

VERIFIED CLIMATE CHANGE

Naturally, an objective observer will acknowledge that our planet's climate is constantly changing—it always has and it always will. If you search historical geological records, you will not find an extended period when the climate remained static. Despite a century of enormously detailed research, climate scientists still do not fully understand the earth's changing weather patterns.

The media's alarmism regarding changes in levels of greenhouse gases and the average global temperature is based largely on an unspoken assumption that there is an ideal global temperature. It follows that any rise or fall of the average global temperature is cause for alarm and calls for enormous political, economic, and lifestyle changes. The stated goal of the flawed man-made global-warming theory is *that we need to act now* to bring the earth's climate back to a mythical "perfect normal temperature."

The expectation that there is an ideal temperature for the earth displays a fundamental lack of scientific understanding. The climate is an enormously complex, dynamic, constantly changing system influenced by the sun, the moon, volcanic activity, and other natural factors that impact our planet's climate.

God created the earth with a marvelously fine-tuned "thermostat." The climate system acts as a sort of planetary thermostat that responds to significant heating or cooling to keep the earth's average temperature within a relatively limited range. This system protects the life of plants, animals, and humanity, and allows them to flourish regardless of the widely different types of local climate that exist—from the frigid Arctic to the scorching heat of the Sahara Desert.

Subsequent to the Little Ice Age (circa 1850), the earth has gradually warmed by about 1.3°F in 150 years. Also during this period, the sea level rose by approximately twelve inches as ocean waters gradually expanded due to warming. This is well within the normal historical range and has caused no serious problems because we know how to adapt to gradual changes in sea level.

The 1.3°F increase in measured global temperature is consistent with a relatively small reduction in solar radiation and the reduction of oceanic clouds. A small reduction in cloud cover over the 70 percent of the earth that is covered by oceans facilitated the gradual warming of the oceans, which in turn warms the atmosphere over the sea. The increased evaporation allows the air to become more humid. As warmer, more humid air flows from the oceans toward land masses, the air slightly increases the atmospheric temperature over the continents. This is the likely cause of most of the global warming that climatologists have measured during the last century and a half.

Neither the gradual rise of average temperatures nor the gradual rise of sea levels has presented a threat of significant disaster. While politicians such as Al Gore and climate activists from the United Nations Intergovernmental Panel on Climate Change (IPCC) claim that rising sea levels are a direct result of man-made global warming, the truth is that sea levels have been increasing steadily by about one foot per century since the last major ice age, which ended ten thousand years ago. The major cause of the rise of sea levels is the gradual expansion of water as solar radiation warms and expands the volume of the oceans.

In light of the fact that the earth was gradually coming out of the Little Ice Age, which lasted some five hundred years from approximately 1350 until 1850, we would expect that the earth's climate would gradually warm back toward equilibrium. However, we must always remember that as a dynamic system, the climate is subject to an extraordinary number of influences. These include ever-changing sun cycles, volcanic eruptions containing greenhouse gases, and the little-understood impact of the El Niño and La Niña currents in the Pacific Ocean. In light of the vast amounts of carbon dioxide held in deep ocean sinks (the ocean depths hold more than fifty times the CO_2 in our atmosphere) in both the Atlantic and Pacific Oceans, we are still far from being able to fully understand the complexity of the earth's climate.

Joseph L. Bast, president of the Heartland Institute, summed up the current environmental situation.

Efforts to quickly reduce human greenhouse gas emissions would be costly and would not stop Earth's climate from changing.

Reducing U.S. carbon dioxide emissions to 7 percent below 1990's levels by the year 2012—the target set by the Kyoto Protocol—would require higher energy taxes and regulations causing the nation to lose 2.4 million jobs and $300 billion in annual economic output. Average household income nationwide would fall by $2,700, and state tax revenues would decline by $93.1 billion due to less taxable earned income and sales, and lower property values. Full implementation of the Kyoto Protocol by all participating nations would reduce global temperature in the year 2100 by a mere 0.14 degrees Celsius [0.25 degrees Fahrenheit].[11]

A large number of climate scientists, politicians, educators, and media figures are focused on the impact of the growing amount of man-made CO_2 in the atmosphere. They assert that this factor alone is the true driver of climate change. But carbon dioxide is a very insignificant trace gas in the atmosphere. Much more CO_2 is contained in the earth's crust, the oceans, the soil, and in biological life than exists in the earth's atmosphere. Consider the fact that the amount of CO_2 produced by all human activities (including power plants and transportation) is only 3 percent of the carbon dioxide that is produced annually by the eruption of volcanoes, the oceans, swamps, peat bogs, termites, animals, and so forth. (I will document this in chapter 8.) In other words, even if we were to eliminate all human production of CO_2, the impact on the climate would be negligible.

THE GLOBAL-WARMING PROPAGANDA CAMPAIGN

The global-warming propaganda campaign is designed to advance the socialist-globalist goal of transforming North American and European capitalist, free-enterprise society. The global-warming alarmists know already that the huge costs and intrusive efforts said to be necessary to mitigate global warming are virtually futile (even if their AGW theory was correct).

Dr. Gro Harlem Brundtland, a special United Nations envoy on climate change who also headed up the 1987 UN World Commission on Environment and Development, declared the need to *end* the climate-change debate. She stated, "This discussion is behind us. It's over.... The diagnosis is clear, the science is unequivocal—it's completely immoral, even, to question now, on the basis of what we know, the reports that are out, to question the issue and to question whether we need to move forward at a much stronger pace as humankind to address the issues."[12]

The arrogance of the most extreme supporters of AGW has led them to label dissenting scientists and commentators as ignorant skeptics who are morally equivalent to Holocaust deniers. Remarkably, in a scientific debate that is only two decades old, there have been repeated efforts in several nations to decertify scientists, climatologists, and meteorologists who publicly admit to any serious scientific skepticism regarding the AGW theory. There are widespread rumors of AGW skeptics being denied tenure in their academic positions, facing obstacles to being published, and not being awarded government and foundation grants despite their academic qualifications.

Unprecedented pressure has been used to try to keep the public from being exposed to skeptical scientific writing, speeches, and other dissenting views regarding the global-warming issue. For example, the BBC has run hundreds of programs, commentaries, and special documentaries that are sympathetic to the global-warming theory. However, after UK Channel 4 ran a program called the *The Great Global Warming Swindle,* which presented a small portion of the skeptics' adversarial scientific position, thirty-seven UK scientists did their utmost to have it canceled.[13]

HOW CLIMATE SCIENTISTS STACK THE DECK

Computer climate models are too crude to accurately predict climate change. The earth's climate is an "open system" that reacts to countless influences, many of which are not yet fully understood. The general circulation models (GCMs) used on supercomputers run at the three major climate study centers are the best tools available in the attempt to calculate how changes in carbon dioxide levels and other greenhouse gases might impact future temperature patterns. However, attempting to predict the ultimate outcome of a staggeringly complex open system—without factoring in the influence of clouds and solar radiation—is irresponsible and inevitably leads to false conclusions.

However, the existing computer climate models ignore the impact of CO_2 emissions from volcanoes, even though volcanoes contribute massive amounts of CO_2 to the atmosphere. And although the sun is the major energy engine for the solar system, the computer models do not factor in the influence of solar radiation. The computer climate models focus almost exclusively on the potential influence of increasing levels of carbon dioxide gas in the atmosphere.

The computer models can't accurately predict the weather in one state or city even two weeks into the future. So why should we believe they can accurately predict the globe's climate and average temperature some ninety years from now? All of the IPCC's predictions of global warming are based on computer models, not on measured temperature data from past ages. In order to get the climate models to make future climate predictions that are close to the designers' expectations, computer modelers resort to "flux adjustments" that can be twenty-five times greater than the effect of doubling carbon dioxide concentrations, their supposed key climate trigger for man-made global warming. Richard A. Kerr, a writer for *Science,* says, "Climate modelers have been 'cheating' for so long it's almost become respectable."[14]

Chris Folland of the UK Meteorological Office's Hadley Center declared that levels of carbon dioxide in the atmosphere were not the key factor in motivating the rush to embrace the man-made global-warming agenda. Folland stated, "The data don't matter. We're not basing our recommendations [for reductions in carbon dioxide emissions] upon the data. We're basing them upon the climate models."[15]

THE GLOBAL-WARMING AGENDA OF THIRD WORLD LEADERS

For decades, leaders of the Organization of Petroleum Exporting Countries (OPEC) nations have charged enormous, irresponsible prices to supply the oil necessary to fuel industrial economies in the West. Following the same pattern, leaders of many Third World nations, for the most part either socialist, Communist, or one-party states, decided it was their turn. Why shouldn't the Third World have a chance to drain the West of billions of dollars annually to augment the foreign-aid programs that allow dictators of Third World nations to develop lavish presidential palaces, hide billions of dollars in Swiss bank accounts, and purchase fleets of luxury cars and private jets?

Beginning in the 1970s, leaders of the Third World (the majority of nations forming the United Nations, the World Trade Organization, and other international groups) conceived of a new idea to enhance their wealth. They created a clever political and global-media promotion to establish a gravy train of foreign aid from the West. At countless international conferences and in numerous UN declarations, Third World leaders demanded the creation of a New International Economic Order.[16]

Their fundamental demand was direct, greedy, and audacious. They demanded that the nations of the industrialized West should transfer hundreds of billions of dollars every year to the treasuries of Third World nations and their dictators in the name of equality and, for good measure, as reparations for centuries of colonialism and slavery. Fortunately, President Ronald Reagan and British Prime Minister Margaret Thatcher had the common sense and moral fortitude in the 1980s to reject such bogus claims.

More recently, since the 1990s, Third World leaders have mounted a new campaign, this time centered on a different sort of reparations. They have demanded hundreds of billions of Western tax dollars annually to repay an imaginary "climate debt." Their rationale is that the industrialized West elevated CO_2 levels for decades prior to the industrialization of parts of the Third World. Unfortunately for citizens of the West, the current group of Western political leaders lacks the moral backbone, principles, courage, and leadership skills to resist such false claims to a share of the West's wealth.

Much of the international political support for the 1997 Kyoto Protocol and the more recent 2009 United Nations Climate Change Conference (better known as the Copenhagen climate summit) comes from the leaders of developing nations. They insist that their countries need hundreds of billions of dollars to assist them in developing green policies and industries, to minimize their contribution to future carbon dioxide emissions.

THE BELIEFS OF THOSE BEHIND THE PROPAGANDA

We need to examine the philosophy and underlying political beliefs of those who espouse man-made global-warming alarmism. As we have seen, they are committed to redistributing the world's wealth. Further, we need to examine their hidden agenda to achieve global government through abolishing independent, sovereign national governments. Their underlying belief system is animated by *two fundamental beliefs.*

The first is an attitude that holds that the vast increase of wealth and the rise in the standard of living in industrial nations is inherently bad for the environment. In light of the relentless growth of technology and the desire for prosperity and material goods, many environmentalists believe humanity would be better off and healthier if we embraced a less technological and significantly poorer lifestyle. However, history reveals that we can only begin to solve the profound environmental, health, and economic problems facing humanity through the wise use of technology and the promotion of wealth. These goals are best accomplished with the availability of inexpensive, reliable energy (oil, natural gas, nuclear power, and clean coal) that fuels a rise in the level of public health, economic freedom, and standard of living.

The second underlying belief that appears to motivate global-warming alarmists is a deeply held attitude that the environment is extremely fragile and must be protected from any possible modification by human activity. As a result of global-warming propaganda, many environmentally focused individuals believe the earth's climate is being pushed past an imaginary, never-before-experienced "tipping point." The propagandists want you to believe that we are in danger of accelerating rising global temperatures past a point of no return.

Even in the face of overwhelming scientific evidence that disproves AGW, continuous propaganda has overwhelmed the common sense of millions of Western citizens. If you repeat a lie often enough, no matter how fantastic the claim, people will eventually accept it as truth. The AGW movement has carried out the most successful propaganda campaign since the Nazi "Big Lie" campaign in the years leading up to World War II.

Assisting in selling the lie is the news media. Ross Gelbspan, former editor of the *Boston Globe,* advised journalists to censor the views, research, and studies of AGW skeptics who contradict and disprove global-warming orthodoxy. Gelbspan went even further to suggest as far back as July 2000 that reporters should not even report the arguments made by climate skeptics.

"Not only do journalists not have a responsibility to report what skeptical scientists have to say about global warming, they have a responsibility not to report what these scientists say."[17]

In a speech by then Illinois state senator Barack Obama in 2006, he declared, "All across the world, in every kind of environment and region known to man, increasingly dangerous weather patterns and devastating storms are abruptly putting an end to the long-running debate over whether or not climate change is real. Not only is it real, it's here, and its effects are giving rise to a frighteningly new global phenomenon: the man-made natural disaster."

Obama continued, "The issue of climate change is one that we ignore at our own peril. There may still be disputes about exactly how much we're contributing to the warming of the earth's atmosphere and how much is naturally occurring, but what we can be scientifically certain of is that our continued use of fossil fuels is pushing us to a point of no return. And unless we free ourselves from a dependence on these fossil fuels and chart a new course on energy in this country, we are condemning future generations to global catastrophe."[18]

Professor Paul Ehrlich, who falsely predicted global famine due to runaway population growth in his 1968 book *The Population Bomb,* is an enthusiastic cheerleader for AGW. Ehrlich declared, "A massive campaign must be launched to de-develop the United States. De-development means bringing our economic system into line with the realities of ecology and the world resource situation."[19]

A revealing statement by Michael Oppenheimer, member of the Environmental Defense Fund, underscores the cynical political agenda behind AGW. Oppenheimer stated, "The only hope for the world is to make sure there is not another United States. We can't let other countries have the same number of cars, the amount of industrialization, we have in the U.S. We have to stop these Third World countries right where they are."[20]

And if those quotes are not troubling enough, here is an open admission regarding the one-world-government agenda of the globalists who are behind the global-warming deception. In reading the 1994 United Nations Human Development Report, I was shocked to read the Special Contribution titled "Global Governance for the 21st Century." This statement was authored by the winner of the 1969 Nobel Prize for economics, Jan Tinbergen:

> Mankind's problems can no longer be solved by national governments. What is needed is a World Government.
>
> This can best be achieved by strengthening the United Nations system. In some cases, this would mean changing the role of UN agencies from advice-giving to implementation....
>
> But some of the most important new institutions would be financial—a World Treasury and a World Central Bank....
>
> Just as each nation has a system of income redistribution, so there should be a corresponding "world financial policy" to be implemented by the World Bank and the World Central Bank....
>
> Some of these proposals are, no doubt, far-fetched and beyond the horizon of today's political possibilities. But the idealists of today often turn out to be the realists of tomorrow.[21]

In the balance of this book we will examine the weak and insufficient scientific "evidence" supporting the theory of man-made global warming. We will also look at the overwhelming scientific evidence that proves that in the past there have been numerous times when the level of atmospheric carbon dioxide has significantly exceeded the present level. This occurred long before the Industrial Revolution, which began to increase humanity's contribution of carbon dioxide into the atmosphere.

Global Warming's False Claims and Flawed Science

onight Show host Jay Leno commented on the onslaught of ever-more-alarming global-warming claims. "According to a new United Nations report," he joked, "the global warming outlook is much worse than originally predicted. Which is pretty bad when you remember they originally predicted it would destroy the planet."[1]

We can all agree that climate change is real. The earth's climate changes constantly in response to terrestrial and extraterrestrial influences. These include solar rays, cosmic rays, massive amounts of space dust, radiation from supernovas (exploding stars in our galaxy), the moon, and numerous other factors. History has recorded significant changes in global temperature dating back to the days of Christ. Epochs of climate change include the Roman Warm Period (250 BC–AD 450), the Medieval Warm Period (900–1300), the Little Ice Age (1350–1850), and gradual warming that took place from the mid-1800s until 1997. During that century and a half, the temperature increased by 1.3°F.

Since 1998 there has been no measurable increase in global temperature, but rather a minor cooling. This is true in spite of the fact that the level of atmospheric carbon dioxide (CO_2) continues to increase.

The small increase in temperature from 1860 to 1997 is a normal recovery of planetary climate equilibrium following the cooling of the Little Ice Age. The gradual temperature increase over nearly 150 years provided ample time for humanity to adapt to a slightly warmer environment without causing significant problems.

THREE CLIMATE-CHANGE QUESTIONS

There are three questions that must be answered by anyone who is concerned about climate change:

1. To what degree has the small measurable rise in global temperature been caused by the normal variation of the climate through natural processes? Conversely, how much is attributable to humanity's increased use of fossil fuels?

2. How severe will the rise in global temperature be during the rest of this century?

3. What reasonable political, social, and economic policies should we pursue to deal with the consequences of a continued rise in global temperature over this century, if this should occur?

While verified climate change is minimal, global-warming alarmists continue to demand massive changes in our society, economy, and lifestyles to deal with the perceived threat of massive anthropogenic global warming (AGW). They propose that in response to their claims that man-made global warming endangers the earth's millions of species, including humanity, we must deconstruct our industrial society, reduce our standard of living, and accept huge increases in income taxes and enormous new energy and carbon taxes. Simultaneously, they insist that we must agree to transfer hundreds of billions of taxpayers' dollars every year out of the U.S. treasury to Third World leaders to pay for a kind of "climate debt."

It has been reported that President Abraham Lincoln declared that: (1) "You can fool some of the people all of the time," and (2) "You can fool all the people some of the time." However, Lincoln also observed that (3) "You can't fool all of the people all the time." AGW supporters are focused on points 1 and 2, but they seem to have forgotten the truth of point 3.

THE ZEAL OF AGW SUPPORTERS

Supporters of the man-made global-warming movement are so zealous that some have admitted they feel justified in exaggerating the dangers. They believe they are justified in using any propaganda claims (including deception) to motivate the news media, business leaders, citizens, and most of all, politicians to take drastic action.

Sir John Houghton was the first co-chairman of the United Nations Intergovernmental Panel on Climate Change (IPCC) and the lead editor of the first three IPCC climate reports. Houghton was quoted in 2008 as follows: "Unless we announce disasters no one will listen." He also warned that the climate danger was greater than the threat of terrorism: "The impacts of global warming are like a weapon of mass destruction."[2] Paul Watson, co-founder of Greenpeace, revealed the deeply cynical attitude of those who support AGW. "It doesn't matter what is true, it only matters what people believe is true."[3] Watson finally resigned from Greenpeace because he felt that Marxists and globalists had subverted the environmental movement.

Christine Stewart, the Liberal Party cabinet member who served as the Canadian Environment Minister (1997–99), revealed that the underlying political motive for radical environmental policies had little to do with the supposed dangers of rising global temperatures. In an interview with the editorial board of the *Calgary Herald,* Stewart revealed that politicians embrace the global-warming cause not because they are convinced that the findings of climate science are settled, but because it is an effective way to achieve their real goal—social engineering. Stewart declared, "No matter if the science is all phony,…there are collateral environmental benefits.… Climate change [provides] the greatest chance to bring about justice and equality in the world."[4] This is an open admission that the AGW cause is little more than a public-relations pretext to achieve, without a public vote, the AGW movement's socialist-globalist agenda.

The stakes are too high for the public to simply give in to a deceptive, alarmist public-relations campaign. It is incumbent on the leaders of the AGW movement to provide in-depth scientific evidence to support their claims. Remember this vital principle: *Extraordinary claims require extraordinary evidence.* In addition, they should engage in open and ongoing scientific debate with those who express serious doubts regarding the global-warming dogma. If global warming does pose a significant danger to humanity, it is vital that we debate the scientific evidence and skeptically examine the climate theory. However, the opposite has happened. AGW supporters such as Al Gore and the United Nations arrogantly claim "the debate is over" and "the science is settled." However, they are contradicting the fundamental nature of true science, which is "the science is never settled." Genuine science is always open to new evidence and new theories, while existing theories are constantly tested against newly discovered evidence.

Timothy Wirth, a former U.S. senator and current president of the United Nations Foundation, revealed the true agenda behind the AGW movement's exaggerated claims of global warming. "We've got to ride this global warming issue. Even if the theory of global warming is wrong, we will be doing the right thing in terms of economic and environmental policy."[5]

PREVIOUS FALSE CLAIMS OF ENVIRONMENTAL CATASTROPHE

To place the AGW deception in perspective, it is worthwhile to examine earlier environmental propaganda campaigns that proved to be both unscientific and fraudulent.

The coming ice age

The *New York Times* created the world's first climate-disaster propaganda campaign in 1895, responding to reports of advancing glaciers and unusually cold weather reports from many nations. The article, titled "Geologists Think the World May Be Frozen Up Again," raised the question of whether "recent and long-continued observations do not point to the advent of a second glacial period."[6]

In 1912, the (London) *Times* reawakened global-cooling fears with a front-page article titled "Prof. Schmidt Warns Us of an Encroaching Ice Age." Cornell University professor N. Schmidt claimed that the world needed "to combat the perils" of the approaching ice age.[7] A decade later, the *Chicago Tribune* ran a front-page article under this headline: "Scientists Say Arctic Ice Will Wipe Out Canada."[8]

Another coming ice age

In the mid-1970s, after three decades of cooling despite rising levels of CO_2 in the air, the new, alarming climate crisis was global cooling. In 1974, *Time* magazine warned of the approaching danger of an unstoppable ice age.[9] Many other newspapers and magazines, including *Newsweek,* announced the impending global freeze in bold headlines. Numerous false claims of approaching environmental disasters were made, accompanied by demands for expensive and urgent solutions.[10]

On the first Earth Day in 1970, prominent environmentalist Kenneth E. F. Watt spoke about the rising threat to humanity from air pollution and global cooling. Watt declared, "If present trends continue, the world will be about 4 degrees colder for the global mean temperature in 1990, but 11 degrees colder by the year 2000. This is about twice what it would take to put us into an ice age."[11]

Not to be outdone, Professor Paul Ehrlich also declared on that day, "In ten years all important animal life in the sea will be extinct. Large areas of coastline will have to be evacuated because of the stench of dead fish."[12] Ehrlich also wrote in 1970, "Five years is all we have left if we are going to preserve any kind of quality in the world."[13]

In 1975, *Science News* published a wonderfully inventive illustration showing New York City covered by an enormous glacier, with the headline "The Ice Age Cometh."[14]

The so-called deadly threat of PCBs

Another threat identified and widely publicized by environmental groups in the 1970s was the danger posed by the widespread use of polychlorinated biphenyls (PCBs). For three decades, PCBs were used in electrical equipment to take advantage of their excellent insulating properties. A researcher from the Centers for Disease Control, Dr. Renate Kimbrough, conducted an experiment in which she fed massive quantities of PCBs to lab rats. Not surprisingly, she found that when rats ingest such huge quantities of PCBs, most of them develop liver cancer. In 1976, Congress banned the use of PCBs.[15]

Remarkably, the same researcher, Renate Kimbrough, completed a new peer-based study twenty-five years later. The study involved seven thousand subjects who had been exposed to massive amounts of PCBs for thirty-one years while working in General Electric power plants. Kimbrough reported that she found no link whatsoever between the workers' long-term exposure to PCBs and their subsequent health problems.[16]

Despite the lack of credible evidence that PCBs were harmful, the Environmental Protection Agency (EPA) spent $780 million to dredge the Hudson River to remove PCBs from the riverbed. Although the dredging operation disturbed the riverbed and therefore significantly *raised* the levels of PCBs, the EPA advised the public there was no danger. If there was no danger, why would the government spend $780 million to remove PCBs? The answer is that politicians care very little about the scientific nature of the problems citizens face. Mostly, members of Congress want to be seen to be "doing something." They are committed to appearing to care about voters and their concerns about the environment. A politician's number-one job, once elected, is to be reelected. Politicians wish to be seen devoting taxpayer money to solve problems, whether the problem actually exists or not.

Paul Ehrlich's population bomb—a dud!

For many years radical environmentalists have presented the most outrageous pseudoscientific predictions, including the dangers from electromagnetic fields and Paul Ehrlich's infamous "population bomb." Ehrlich's 1968 book *The Population Bomb* warned that the growing global population was creating unsupportable pressures on the earth's food supply and on limited natural resources. He noted that, while food production and the processing of resources grows linearly over time, the global population was expanding geometrically. As a result, he concluded that global famine and economic collapse were inevitable.

However, humanity's ability to discover and develop inexpensive new energy sources, including gas and oil, clean coal, and nuclear power, has out-paced the growth in population. Further, food resources are growing much faster than the population, partially due to the enhanced growth rates of al-most all plants in the presence of rising levels of CO_2 in the atmosphere. It is significant that the global-warming alarmists almost never mention the posi-tive benefits that agricultural production derives from additional CO_2 in the atmosphere, which forms an important nutrient for all plants.

The United Nations has pointed out that the rate of population increase has moderated significantly over the last three decades as women in the Third World, including the Islamic nations, have fewer children. (This is due to education, access to contraception, the spread of women's rights, and rising family income.) However, you will not be surprised to discover that Ehrlich has now embraced a new threat to humanity—the deadly danger of man-made global warming. Meanwhile, past global dangers from climate cooling, PCBs, and a runaway population no longer appear in the speeches and writ-ings of climate alarmists.

The global ban on DDT and resulting deaths due to malaria

DDT, the most effective antimalarial pesticide in history, was virtually pro-hibited by government decree as a result of irresponsible environmental alarm-ism. For decades, civilians and military personnel alike fought the spread of malaria-bearing mosquitoes with DDT. There was no scientific evidence that DDT was harmful to humans, while the obvious effectiveness of DDT to control mosquitoes was proven. The use of DDT eliminated malaria from North America and Europe.

The unwarranted ban on DDT came in response to novelist-naturalist Rachel Carson's 1962 book *Silent Spring.* Her book suggested (without scien-tific evidence) that DDT would kill all birds, hence the book's title. In 1972, the EPA reacted to the public response to Carson's *Silent Spring* by forbidding the use of DDT in the United States. Later the USA demanded that all Third World nations receiving foreign aid from the United States eliminate the use of DDT. Those nations were forced to replace the banned pesticide with a much more expensive—and much less effective—alternative. Tragically, during the last five decades, according to Robert Gwadz of the National Institutes of Health, twenty million children have died needlessly due to exposure to malaria.[17]

However, after five decades and tens of millions of easily avoidable malaria-related deaths in Africa and the Third World, *New York Times* columnist Nicholas Kristof endorsed the resumption of the widespread use of DDT to combat the spread of mosquitoes that transmit malaria.[18] Carson's antipesticide gospel is no longer sacrosanct, even with the liberal media.[19]

IS AGW IMPOSSIBLE TO *DISPROVE*?

It is a curious but very noteworthy feature of the man-made global-warming theory that it is not "falsifiable." A legitimate scientific theory makes a prediction about the consequences that will follow certain conditions. Then the theory is tested to verify whether the theory is true or false. However, the theory of man-made global warming as presented by its political and scientific supporters is incapable of being proved true or false. Genuine scientific theories must be falsifiable, but there is no global climate experiment that can be done to test this theory.

According to the AGW alarmists, unseasonable warm weather *and* unusual cold weather can both be cited as compelling evidence in support of the global-warming theory. No matter what the weather trends indicate, a hypothetical model of global warming will be brought forth to offer a confident explanation. This reveals a profound weakness in the theory of man-made global warming.

U.S. Senator James M. Inhofe, the leading Republican on the Committee on Environment and Public Works, has issued warnings regarding the dangers posed by the AGW movement. "With all of the hysteria, all of the fear, all of the phony science, could it be that man-made global warming is the greatest hoax ever perpetrated on the American people? It sure sounds like it."[20]

Ian Plimer, in his book *Heaven and Earth,* discusses scientific findings about CO_2 levels in long ages past.

Geologists have measured the global temperatures and CO_2 levels in the ancient past by examining the chemical composition of the air bubbles in the ice cores from Antarctica and Greenland. To their surprise they found that the atmospheric CO_2 levels during several of the ancient ice ages were significantly higher than we experience today. The very cold Ordovician-Silurian ice age occurred approximately 450 to 420 million years ago when the CO_2 level was 4000 ppmv [parts per million by volume]. The Jurassic-Cretaceous ice age happened approximately 130 million years ago when the atmosphere contained 2000 ppmv (five times higher than we experience today).[21]

Increased global temperatures from 1860 until the late 1990s were caused primarily by increased solar radiation and not by increased levels of CO_2. Rising levels of CO_2 historically *follow* by many centuries the rise of global temperatures. This disproves the AGW theory. Research has confirmed that higher global atmospheric temperatures produce an increase in the level of atmospheric carbon dioxide. Here's why. The oceans contain more than fifty times the CO_2 that is contained in the atmosphere. Therefore, the higher the global temperature produced by solar radiation and other natural causes, the more likely it is that the oceans will release an increased amount of CO_2 into the air.

Massive amounts of CO_2 held in deep ocean sinks are released into the atmosphere—and years later are reabsorbed into the oceans. The oceans will, with warmer water temperature, cause the continued release of CO_2 into the atmosphere.[22]

GUESSING AT THE ENVIRONMENT'S FUTURE

Weather forecasters and meteorologists, using the most sophisticated computerized weather models, admit that weather forecasts are fairly accurate for a maximum of one week. Weather forecasts, even when they are limited to local areas, are open to great error if the prediction extends to ten days. Therefore, it is remarkable to consider the absolute certainty of AGW climate predictions *for the year 2100.* One of the most effective propaganda arguments used by global-warming alarmists refers to the threat of rising sea levels. It's an effective device for two reasons. First, who would not want to prevent Baltimore, San Diego, or Miami from being inundated by rising seas? Second, in the hands of a propagandist, the idea of rising sea levels can be graphically and convincingly portrayed. It's like a science fiction movie that is presented as a factual science documentary.

AGW warnings about rising sea levels have international implications. In only a few decades, they claim, we could lose much of Singapore and even New York City. Consider the threat to the lowland countries of Europe. Rising sea levels would be a global catastrophe. And beyond the massive loss of property and human life, we would lose enormous numbers of animal species whose habitats would be obliterated.

Initially, the scientific evidence supporting claims of future rising sea levels and the damage that would be caused appeared credible. But a closer look reveals serious problems. The IPCC predictions of significant rises in sea levels and enormous loss of species are based on a spurious scientific methodology. A number of respected scientists have criticized the IPCC's methodology as being fundamentally flawed, saying it is virtually guaranteed to produce a significant *overestimate* of biological species loss due to global warming

HUMAN ACTS AND GLOBAL WARMING

Those who promote the man-made global-warming theory argue that carbon dioxide emissions due to human activities are primarily responsible for contributing to the greenhouse effect, thus warming the earth's atmosphere. Research reveals that CO_2 levels have varied markedly over thousands of years—long before humanity's significant production of CO_2 from the burning of fossil fuels.

Since the 1880s, the CO_2 content of the atmosphere has increased. The annual growth rate of CO_2 in the atmosphere doubled from 0.2 percent per year to the present rate of approximately 0.4 percent per year. However, the 0.4 percent annual growth has been stable for twenty-five years. And there is no absolute scientific proof that humanity's increasing contributions of CO_2 to the atmosphere are the main driver of global warming.[23]

Core sample measurements of ice in Greenland and Antarctica reveal accurate historical temperatures dating back thousands of years. Scientists were surprised to find that atmospheric CO_2 levels increased significantly many years—and even centuries—*after* global temperatures had increased.

It is the increase in global temperature—caused primarily by variations in levels of solar radiation, variations in the water cycle (primarily the degree of cloud cover), and variations in the earth's orbital position—that causes a delayed increase in the amount of CO_2 in the atmosphere. *Global temperature controls the amount of carbon dioxide in the atmosphere, not the other way around.*[24]

Seas and oceans also play a role. Increased warming impacts the surface layers of the oceans, causing the water to release much more CO_2 into the atmosphere. When ocean temperatures rise, the warm water "outgasses," or releases, much more carbon dioxide into the atmosphere. In addition, carbon dioxide is more soluble in cold water. When the oceans are cooler, they absorb much more carbon dioxide from the atmosphere. There is a constant interchange of CO_2 between the oceans' CO_2 sinks and the atmosphere.[25]

A FASTER RATE OF WARMING?

Another global-warming myth is that global temperatures are rising at an unprecedented rate. But thousands of accurate scientific measurements, beginning with satellite deployment in 1979, have failed to reveal any significant change in the long-term rate of increase in global temperatures. While average temperature readings from ground stations reveal a slight warming of just more than 1°F over the last century, this temperature variation is well within the natural climate variations identified during the last millennium.

However, even the small temperature increase documented in the last century is uncertain because of the variable accuracy of the ground-station temperature network, which suffers from the fact that many of the sensors are located in "urban heat islands." These are urban and industrial areas that show substantially higher readings than the surrounding rural areas. Many temperature sites were originally located in rural areas, which have gradually been surrounded by buildings, parking lots, and roads. Development artificially increases the temperature readings because concrete and asphalt absorb and hold heat better than trees and grass. When adjusted for the artificial urban-heat-island effect, much of the proclaimed rise in land temperatures during the last century can be discounted.[26]

DELIBERATE AGW DECEPTION

Historical and scientific evidence strongly supports the fact that the earth has undergone numerous major climate changes. Humanity experienced a major warming of the climate in the centuries of the Medieval Warm Period, between AD 900 and 1300. This warming period occurred centuries before the Industrial Revolution and humanity's increased production of greenhouse gases. The Medieval Warm Period was followed by a long cooling period known as the Little Ice Age.

Very little scientific evidence exists to prove that CO_2 has more than a slight moderating effect on global temperature. And since 1998, despite continuing contributions of man-made CO_2, we have experienced significant global cooling of almost 1°F. Almost all the global warming since 1900, equal to slightly more than 1°F, has since been erased by recent cooling. *Yet none of the computer models that forecast future climate change predicted the recent period of global cooling, nor do they account for it.*[27]

Thus, the alarming climate scenarios that AGW proponents predict for the years 2050 and 2100 cannot be proven based on current temperature readings or historical climate research. The climate-change scenarios issued by the United Nations Intergovernmental Panel on Climate Change (IPCC) are not based on temperature research, but on complex computer models. To try to prove that their computer models are accurate, they have two choices:

1. Compare recent climatic trends to actual temperature records
2. Compare recent climatic trends to historic thermometer readings as well as climate records inferred from other sources. Those sources include Greenland and Antarctic ice core samples, ocean seabed sediments, and tree rings. These sources are known generically as *proxy data*.

The problem with the first approach is that humans have been recording temperatures across the globe for only the last century and a half. Many of the temperature records are inaccurate or incomplete. And in terms of natural climatic fluctuations, a century and a half is much too short a period to use as the basis for reaching reliable scientific conclusions. So scientists were left with proxy temperature data.

When the IPCC issued its first report, the committee responsible was confronted with an embarrassing problem. The proxy data showed that the earth's most recent warming trend isn't all that unusual. Specifically, proxy data showed that during the Medieval Warm Period, the earth's temperature was much higher than it is today. If CO_2 emissions resulting from human activities are the primary cause of global warming, then global warming enthusiasts now need to explain what caused significant warming (2°F) during the centuries of the Medieval Warm Period.

With serious questions arising related to the IPCC's climate-change reports, a number of scholars and scientists from various disciplines studied the IPCC data and uncovered major flaws in both the methodology and in the conclusions. Long-term temperature studies reveal that since the end of the Little Ice Age in 1860, the warmest decade recorded was not the 1990s, as claimed by global-warming alarmists, but the 1930s. The 1930s predate the era when the levels of man-made contributions of CO_2 to the atmosphere began to rise significantly.[28]

IPCC researchers refer to their work as "science." However, in too many instances to count, their work has been shown to be nothing more than science fiction and propaganda. In chapter 7, we will examine additional evidence of deliberately falsified climate data.

Fatal Flaws in the Official Global-Warming Documents

The global-warming movement was born in 1988 as a result of growing concerns that an accelerated increase in global temperatures could negatively impact humans and animals. In 1989, the United Nations Environment Program (UNEP) joined with the World Meteorological Organization (WMO) to create the Intergovernmental Panel on Climate Change (IPCC).

Scientists previously had attributed changes in the earth's climate primarily to the activity and effects of the sun. However, global-warming scientists started promoting the theory that a gradual increase in temperature (1.3°F since 1860) was not simply a gradual recovery from the cooling of the Little Ice Age. Instead, climate scientists developed a theory that the earth's temperature had started rising much more rapidly as a consequence of humanity's growing use of fossil fuels. Liberal-socialist political leaders, together with liberal-left allies in the scientific community, identified the environment's new enemy: carbon dioxide. They argued that man-made production of carbon dioxide (CO_2), primarily in the industrialized West, was a growing threat to the survival of the human race.

Climate experts from many nations began assembling official reports on global warming to update world leaders on what the scientists said was verifiable climate change. Every few years, the UN presents these combined scientific findings in a summary to the world's top political leaders. The IPCC issued comprehensive climate assessments in 1990, 1995, 2001, and 2007.

The most recent report, referred to as AR4 (the Fourth Assessment Report), looked at the climate-change projections of twenty-three computer models. The IPCC-approved computer models promote the theory that the earth's temperature will rise from as little as 1.1°C (2.0°F) to as much as 6.4°C (11.5°F) between now and the year 2100. That is a remarkably wide variation. AR4 strongly supported the UN plan to globalize the world's economy, including privately owned corporations, in an attempt to reduce the use of fossil fuels in the production of energy and consumer products.

Although *precise temperature readings made by satellites since 1979 reveal zero warming of the earth's surface temperatures,*[1] and *the latest underwater sensors reveal no rising temperatures in the oceans,*[2] those who embrace global-warming hysteria declare repeatedly that "the science of global warming is settled." They insist there is no reason for further debate, even though their proposed solution requires spending hundreds of billions of dollars every year for the next century. Their solution also involves the massive restriction and dislocation of numerous human economic endeavors.

In fact, a fundamental assumption in science is that "science is never settled." Genuine science requires that we constantly reevaluate previous hypotheses, theories, and conclusions in light of new scientific evidence. When considering the scientific basis for the theory that undergirds anthropogenic global warming (AGW), it's vital to remember that any scientific hypothesis can be invalidated by a single piece of new, absolutely verifiable, contradictory evidence. True science is always open to the discovery of new evidence, the revision of current theories, and the development and exploration of new theories.

The global-warming hypothesis predicts that global temperatures will rise in direct ratio to the rise of man-made carbon dioxide added to the earth's atmosphere. But this AGW theory has already been contradicted by a gradual decline in global temperatures since 1998,[3] while CO_2 levels continue to rise. Significantly, not one of the two dozen computer models that form the foundation of the IPCC's prevailing theory of man-made global warming predicted the cooling that the earth has experienced since 1998.[4]

Indeed, there is more than sufficient reason to question public statements of global-warming scientists and researchers. A substantial number of the panel of twenty-five hundred climate scientists on the IPCC, which created a statement on scientific "unanimity" on man-made global warming, were found to privately maintain *serious concerns* about the report's conclusions. The Nongovernmental International Panel on Climate Change concluded, "We find no support for the IPCC's claim that climate observations during the twentieth century are either unprecedented or provide evidence of an anthropogenic effect on climate."[5]

LOOKING INSIDE THE IPCC

There has never been an open scientific debate on the AGW theory. The global-warming alarmists simply insist that historical temperature data proves that rising levels of CO_2 in the air raises global temperatures. The IPCC is not a large United Nations organization. It has only ten full-time staff in its secretariat at the WMO in Geneva, Switzerland, plus a few staff in four technical support units that assist the chairs of the three IPCC working groups and the national greenhouse-gas inventories group. The lion's share of the IPCC's work is done by unpaid volunteers, the thousands of scientists at universities and research institutions around the world who contribute as authors or reviewers to the completion of the official IPCC reports.

Scientists from the other side of the debate weigh in

In August 2007, a comprehensive survey of peer-reviewed scientific literature from 2004 to 2007 revealed that fewer than 50 percent of all "published scientists" endorse the AGW theory. "Of 539 total papers on climate change, only 38 (7%) gave an explicit endorsement of the consensus. If one considers 'implicit' endorsement (accepting the consensus without explicit statement), the figure rises to 45%. However, while only 32 papers (6%) reject the consensus outright, the largest category (48%) are neutral papers, refusing to either accept or reject the hypothesis."[6]

This finding contradicts official statements of the National Academy of Sciences (NAS) and the American Meteorological Society (AMS), which have endorsed the so-called consensus view that humanity's contribution of CO_2 to the atmosphere is driving global warming. But what you don't hear is that both the NAS and AMS leadership never allowed member scientists to vote on the official climate statements.[7] Only fifty-two scientists participated in formulating the IPCC summary report released in 2007. The notion that "hundreds" or "thousands" of UN climate scientists agree to the IPCC's official stance on global warming is not supported by evidence.

Professor Pat Finnegan, a senior Irish member of the IPCC, admitted that he had not bothered to read the fourth IPCC report (AR4) in its entirety because "it was over 1800 pages long."[8] But he still advocates changing our lifestyle based on the report's findings. Finnegan is a member of Working

Group III (WG3), the IPCC mitigation panel that deals with the impact of global warming on humans and animals.

The need for an open global-warming debate

It is vital that a complete scientific analysis and debate take place that examines all the evidence behind the global-warming agenda. The leaders who promote AGW and its political-economic agenda want nothing less than to force the United States and Europe to surrender to a socialistic, Marxist, and globalist agenda. Their ultimate goal is to create a global government led by an elite group using an environmental agenda to convince sovereign nations to surrender their freedom and political independence. The globalists insist that the extreme dangers posed by AGW require drastic action.

However, recent studies and new climate research conducted by world-class climate scholars are repudiating the alarmist claims of Al Gore–style global-warming activists. As just one example, *a climate study published in the scientific journal* Nature *found no relationship whatsoever between the levels of CO_2 in the atmosphere and global temperatures over long geological time periods.*[9]

IPCC EVASIONS AND THE FALSIFICATION OF DATA

The next IPCC report will be released in 2013. Critics of AGW will be eager to see if by then the IPCC chooses to utilize valid data on the earth's temperature throughout history. Very few of the climate predictions included in the IPCC's 2001 report were based on reliable historical evidence from thermometer readings recorded since 1850. Nor were they based on precise satellite temperature measurements made since 1979. Instead, the major driver of the conclusions presented in the 2001 IPCC report are complex computer models that are simply scenarios of possible climate trends and outcomes.

Computer models are mathematical projections, and anyone who has dealt with computer programs knows the programming truism: garbage in, garbage out (GIGO). In other words, the end results are only as accurate as the programming itself and the data that is input. A climate computer model tells us much more about the computer programmer's fundamental assumptions than it does about the earth's climate in the year 2100.

As just one example, the five computer-model predictions created by universities selected to participate in an early IPCC report all predicted that global temperature would continue to increase every year from 1990 through 1995 and onward.[10] As the carbon dioxide level rose each year, the computer models projected that the temperature would also increase every year. However, while the level of carbon dioxide continued to increase, the global temperature stopped increasing by 1998, at which time the temperature began to gradually drop. The underlying global-warming scenarios are not borne out by actual temperature readings.

The mathematical computer modeling of any tremendously complex and open system such as the earth's climate is merely theoretical. Computer models indicate potential scenarios; they do not constitute scientific evidence in themselves. It is astonishing, then, that the IPCC is allowed to issue flawed and misleading reports that are used to attack our independence, our free-enterprise economy, and our standard of living. The ugly truth is that many environmental activists want to eliminate our economic and political freedom in favor of an extreme form of socialist global government.

CLIMATE SCIENTISTS LAMBAST IPCC METHODOLOGY

All of the supercomputer climate models predicted that rising CO_2 levels would result in a hot zone in the mid-troposphere, but it has not happened. (The troposphere is the lowest level of earth's atmosphere, four to eleven miles from the ground.) Dr. Steven M. Japar is an atmospheric chemist who was part of the IPCC's Second (1995) and Third (2001) Assessment Reports. He has authored eighty-three peer-reviewed publications in the areas of climate change, atmospheric chemistry, air pollution, and vehicle emissions. Japar wrote, "Temperature measurements show that the [climate-model-predicted mid-troposphere] hot zone is non-existent. This is more than sufficient to invalidate global climate models and projections made with them!"[11]

"The claims of the IPCC are dangerous unscientific nonsense," according to IPCC reviewer and climate researcher Dr. Vincent Gray of New Zealand. Gray was an expert reviewer on every draft of the IPCC reports going back to 1990 and is the author of more than one hundred scientific publications.[12]

Dr. John Brignell, an emeritus engineering professor who held the chair in Industrial Instrumentation at the University of Southampton, accused the United Nations of censorship on July 23, 2008. Brignell wrote,

Here was a purely political body posing as a scientific institution. Through the power of patronage it rapidly attracted acolytes. Peer review soon rapidly evolved from the old style refereeing to a much more sinister imposition of The Censorship.... New circles of like-minded propagandists formed, acting as judge and jury for each other. Above all, they acted in concert to keep out alien and hostile opinion. "Peer review" developed into a mantra that was picked up by political activists who clearly had no idea of the procedures of science or its learned societies. It became an imprimatur of political acceptability, whose absence was equivalent to placement on the proscribed list.[13]

Research by Australian climate-data analyst John McLean revealed that the IPCC's peer-review process is "an illusion." McLean found that very few scientists publicly support the central IPCC assertion that increased greenhouse gases have been the dominant cause of global warming over the last fifty years. "The reality is that there is surprisingly little explicit support for this key notion. Among the 23 independent reviewers just 4 explicitly endorsed the chapter with its hypothesis, and one other endorsed only a specific section. Moreover, only 62 of the IPCC's 308 reviewers commented on this chapter at all."[14]

Please note that only five scientists out of twenty-three reviewers in the IPCC peer-review process explicitly endorsed the key chapter (or a portion of it) blaming humanity for global warming in the past fifty years.

THE ASTOUNDING ERRORS IN IPCC REPORTS

Following is a quick review of what current and former UN-affiliated scientists have said about the IPCC's claimed "very open" process. One former IPCC scientist bluntly told the Senate Committee on Environment and Public Works (EPW) that the IPCC's Summary for Policymakers "distorted" the scientists' work. "I have found examples of a Summary saying precisely the opposite of what the scientists said," explained South African nuclear physicist and chemical engineer Dr. Philip Lloyd, an IPCC co-coordinating lead author.[15]

In an August 13, 2007, letter, Dr. Madhav Khandekar, a retired Environment Canada scientist, lashed out at those who "seem to naively believe that the climate change science espoused in the [UN's] Intergovernmental Panel on Climate Change (IPCC) documents represents 'scientific consensus.'" Khandekar continued, "As one of the invited expert reviewers for the 2007 IPCC documents, I have pointed out the flawed review process used by the IPCC scientists in one of my letters. I have also pointed out in my letter that an increasing number of scientists are now questioning the hypothesis of Greenhouse gas induced warming of the earth's surface and suggesting a stronger impact of solar variability and large-scale atmospheric circulation patterns on the observed temperature increase than previously believed.... Unfortunately, the IPCC climate change documents do not provide an objective assessment of the earth's temperature trends and associated climate change."[16]

Hurricane expert Christopher W. Landsea, of the National Oceanic and Atmospheric Administration (NOAA) National Hurricane Center, was an author and a reviewer for the IPCC's Second Assessment Report in 1995 and the Third Assessment Report in 2001. He resigned from the Fourth Assessment Report after charging the UN with playing politics with hurricane science. Landsea issued a public letter detailing his experience with the UN: "I am withdrawing [from the UN] because I have come to view the part of the IPCC to which my expertise is relevant as having become politicized. In addition, when I have raised my concerns to the IPCC leadership, their response was simply to dismiss my concerns.... I personally cannot in good faith continue to contribute to a process that I view as both being motivated by pre-conceived agendas and being scientifically unsound."[17]

A significant statement that was *deleted* from the 1995 IPCC report stated that "none of the studies cited above has shown clear evidence that we can attribute the observed [climate] changes to the specific cause of increases in greenhouse gases."[18] It was deleted because it contradicted the beliefs of those who wrote the final recommendations of the UN report.

Former Colorado State University climatologist Dr. Roger Pielke Sr. also detailed the corruption of the IPCC process.

> The same individuals who are doing primary research in the role of humans on the climate system are then permitted to lead the [IPCC] assessment! There should be an outcry on this obvious conflict of interest, but to date either few recognize this conflict, or see that since

the recommendations of the IPCC fit their policy and political agenda, they chose to ignore this conflict. In either case, scientific rigor has been sacrificed and poor policy and political decisions will inevitably follow.... We need recognition among the scientific community, the media, and policymakers that the IPCC process is obviously a real conflict of interest, and this has resulted in a significantly flawed report.[19]

ADDITIONAL ERRONEOUS AND FALSIFIED CLAIMS

The IPCC Fourth Assessment Report claims that global-warming "impacts on biodiversity are significant and of key relevance."[20] However, those claims are not supported by accepted scientific research. Further, the IPCC's claims that climate change threatens many of the world's species do not make sense. Consider that most wild species are at least one million years old, which means they have been through hundreds of significant climate cycles, from ice ages to significantly warmer periods. Obviously, these species have adapted and survived.

There also is reason to question IPCC assertions regarding the Amazon rain forest. It appears the rain forest research that forms part of the IPCC's 2007 report was produced by nonscientists who wrote for the environmental groups World Wildlife Fund (WWF) and the International Union for Conservation of Nature (IUCN). Upon examination, there is no apparent scientific documentation in the IPCC's 2007 report supporting the claim that up to 40 percent of the Amazon rain forest is threatened by global-warming trends. This deficiency raises serious questions regarding how carefully the IPCC verified the scientific support for the dramatic and fear-inspiring headlines generated from its report.

Included in the report was the following statement: "Up to 40 percent of the Amazonian forests could react drastically to even a slight reduction in precipitation; this means that the tropical vegetation, hydrology and climate system in South America could change very rapidly to another steady state, not necessarily producing gradual changes between the current and the future situation."[21]

The sloppy science and unorthodox documentation behind the AGW movement are troubling to say the least. But the average citizen does not have access to scientific journal articles, the truth about research methodologies, or the computer models that generate climate statistics and projections. So how do we uncover the truth regarding systemic bias in the official IPCC global-warming reports?

It is good to question the leading spokesmen for AGW, and by far the most well-known voice on climate change is that of former U.S. Vice President Al Gore. In the next chapter we will examine many of the deceptions presented in his book *Earth in the Balance* and movie *An Inconvenient Truth*—and what his misrepresentations mean for the world.

Al Gore's Convenient Lies

Former U.S. Vice President Al Gore became an enthusiastic environmentalist some three decades ago. In the years since, he has become the leading exponent of the pagan religion of man-made global warming. Since writing his 1992 book *Earth in the Balance,* Gore has worked overtime to convince the rest of us that humanity's daily activities are destroying the environment. Ordinary things such as burning coal to generate electricity, driving your car to work, or cutting down trees to produce lumber to build homes—all of these actions, we are told, have deadly consequences.

The culprit is the carbon dioxide emissions that are produced by our daily lives. Gore is quick to push for drastic measures to minimize the alleged CO_2 threat, regardless of the massive social, economic, and political costs. He founded the Alliance for Climate Protection, and he is author of *Our Choice: A Plan to Solve the Climate Crisis.* In addition, he is a successful businessman who has promoted a high-profile, global publicity campaign to minimize man-made global warming while profiting financially from efforts to limit CO_2 emissions.

In 2004 Gore cofounded Generation Investment Management to manage carbon-trading credits. On June 30, 2010, Ameritrade stated, "As of June 30, 2010, funds at Generation Investment Management, founded by Al Gore and David Blood, were valued at $2.6 billion."[1]

Gore's book *An Inconvenient Truth* and the related PowerPoint presentation have generated more than $50 million for the author. And he reportedly earns from $100,000 to $150,000 for every lecture he gives on global warming.[2]

He has made enormous amounts of money through huge investments in renewable energy companies and by creating a global-warming trust company, Generation Investment Management. This company issues certificates that enable investors in alternative-energy companies to believe they have helped improve the earth's climate by investing in a "carbon offset" arrangement. In doing so, they can supposedly offset their enormous carbon footprint created by using private jets and other significant uses of energy. Their investments in renewable-energy companies developing "green" energy (generating power without relying on fossil fuels) demonstrate their commitment to saving the earth.

Gore conveniently overlooks the fact that there is an enormous, well-funded, global-warming industry—of which Gore is a significant player. The climate-change industry supports the academics, scientists, nongovernmental organizations, media, and political groups that together promote the anthropogenic global warming (AGW) movement. There is far greater financial support available to those who promote the man-made global-warming agenda than there is for any scientists who dare to explore alternative climate research theories.

GORE'S INTERNATIONAL
GLOBAL-WARMING CAMPAIGN

Gore joined the AGW movement in the 1980s through the tutoring of NASA scientist James Hansen. He became convinced that the only way to preserve humanity from the coming climate disaster would be to lead a worldwide campaign to convince individuals, business leaders, politicians, and world leaders to drastically curtail the production and use of fossil fuels. Of course, doing so would severely reduce our wealth, our standard of living, and our quality of life.

Gore created an illustrated book titled *An Inconvenient Truth,* in which he presented the scientific arguments supporting the theory of AGW. He followed the book with a PowerPoint presentation titled *An Inconvenient Truth,* which has been shown around the globe, including to hundreds of millions of students in classrooms throughout the West. Gore has trained more than a thousand supporters to use this PowerPoint presentation.

Gore's partisan, ideological book and video are presented as objective climate science and moral common sense dealing with what he calls the "planetary emergency of global warming." Gore's presentation unfortunately promotes a remarkable number of false or unsupported claims and reveals little objectivity regarding a very complex scientific, environmental, and political issue.

Curiously, while his book calls for massive cuts in humanity's use of fossil fuels, his book and PowerPoint presentation fail to acknowledge that our use of fossil fuels to produce inexpensive electrical power plays an indispensable role in the West's economic prosperity. Through the use of inexpensive electrical power and the use of petroleum-based fertilizers to increase food production, our effective use of fossil fuels has contributed to the significant lengthening of human life, the provision of numerous consumer goods, our enjoyment of leisure, and inexpensive and reliable transportation. Taken together, these advances have lifted the standard of living of hundreds of millions of Westerners. And the economic and social benefits of fossil-fuel power have been extended to billions of people in the Third World.

It also is a convenient omission that Gore fails to mention that a warmer climate significantly improves the quality of life and general health of humanity. Warmer temperatures benefit agricultural production, which enhances the food supply and national economies. Historical health records demonstrate that the human population (especially the very young and the old) suffer significantly higher death rates from periods of colder weather than from periods of warmer weather. Nor does Gore acknowledge that the continuing rise of CO_2 in the atmosphere enhances the growth rate of many plants, crops, and trees.

The United States is a favorite target of the former vice president, since America is second only to China in producing CO_2 emissions. But this ignores the obvious fact that higher carbon emissions are the inevitable result of a highly productive economy and an extensive transportation system.

Despite a number of scientists and others who have disputed the numerous errors included in *An Inconvenient Truth,* Gore still refuses to debate his critics. Despite many invitations, he has dodged the opportunity to engage in a debate with Lord Christopher Monckton and other thoughtful and informed global-warming critics. Instead of engaging in reasoned discussions, he has demonized anyone who dares to disagree with him. He has often compared his critics to people who believe the earth is flat. "They're almost like the ones who still believe that the moon landing was staged in a movie lot in Arizona and those who believe the earth is flat."[3]

GORE'S CLAIMS OF RISING SEA LEVELS

Gore claims that carbon dioxide in the atmosphere is almost the sole cause of higher global temperatures. He claimed in *An Inconvenient Truth* that in the last four interglacial warming periods, the previous changes in CO_2 concentration in the atmosphere caused a significant rise in global temperatures.[4]

Gore and others who lead the AGW movement insist that global warming will raise sea levels and adversely affect coastal regions. However, their books and speeches overlook the fact that many coastal areas are subject to sinking, which is unrelated to predicted rising sea levels. In a number of instances, including the east coast of England and the coast of Bangladesh, geological factors are producing significant sinking of the land.[5]

This is a geological consequence of isostatic recovery following an ice age, or in the case of Bangladesh, it's a gradual sinking of the land due to long-term tectonic subduction. Of course, local and regional geological shifts have *no relationship* to either global warming or to the theoretical rise in sea levels resulting from increases in CO_2 levels in the atmosphere.

While Gore's claims are supposedly based on the 2007 report of the United Nations Intergovernmental Panel on Climate Change (IPCC), that study suggests only that the possible melting of massive ice sheets in Greenland and western Antarctica would add 2.5 inches (6 cm) to the global sea level over the next one hundred years.[6] Gore's estimate of a rise of 23 feet in the sea level exaggerated the IPCC estimate of 2.5 inches by 10,000 percent. Even the most extreme scenario calculated by the United Nations calls for a maximum rise of two feet by 2100. More surprisingly, the IPCC 2007 report suggests a probability of 50:50 for human activity having *any* effect on sea levels. Further, the IPCC report refers to the possible melting of the ice sheets in Greenland due to the ice sheets' "dynamic ice flow," not because of human activity.[7]

Gore's presentation also makes the claim that the Canadian Arctic Ocean's ice cover has been reduced drastically due to global warming. It is true that the seasonal and annually variable Arctic ice pack had been shrinking for many years (until 1998, when global temperatures started dropping). Meanwhile, the ice shelf and depth of ice in the Antarctic has been growing at a record pace, to the point that in 2007 it reached the highest ice level ever recorded. Most of the previous loss of ice cover in the Arctic has been restored.[8]

Gore's book claims that global warming is endangering the population of polar bears. He stated in *An Inconvenient Truth* that polar bears "have been drowning in significant numbers" due to the loss of Arctic sea ice.[9] However, this assertion was based on nothing more than a single 2005 report that found that four polar bears had drowned in one month. This unusual event occurred during an exceptional storm, with high winds and waves in the Beaufort Sea.[10]

The truth is that the polar bear population has risen almost 500 percent from approximately 5,000 bears in the 1950s to an estimated 23,000-plus bears today.[11] The only real threat to polar bears comes from hunting, which involves issuing licenses each year to both aboriginal natives and wealthy North American trophy hunters. This hunting of polar bears is easily controlled and modified annually through legal restrictions on the number of hunting licenses sold. During the last interglacial period, when global temperatures were 5°C (9°F) warmer than today, polar bears survived without difficulty.[12]

PACIFIC ISLANDS ENDANGERED BY RISING SEAS?

One of Gore's most startling warnings concerns the supposed plight of thousands of Pacific islanders living on low-level islands such as the Maldives and

Tuvalu. Citizens of these islands are demanding that the United Nations, as well as Australia or New Zealand, transport them to safety and provide citizenship in their countries.

Politicians and climate-change campaigners have repeatedly predicted that the tiny multi-island nation of Tuvalu will be overcome by rising seas. The highest point on Tuvalu is only fifteen feet above sea level. However, researchers discovered that seven of Tuvalu's islands have increased in area by more than 3 percent on average since the 1950s. Professor Paul Kench, a geographer, has measured twenty-seven islands where local sea levels have risen almost five inches over the past sixty years and found that only four of the islands had diminished in size. Remarkably, the remaining twenty-three islands had either remained unchanged or had expanded in area, according to the research published in the journal *Global and Planetary Change*. Scientific evidence suggests that the islands respond to modifications in weather patterns and climate. For example, in 1972 Cyclone Bebe deposited 140 hectares (346 acres) of sediment on the eastern reef of Tuvalu, thus increasing the main island's total area by 10 percent.[13]

Dr. Nils-Axel Mörner is a Swedish geologist and physicist and the former chairman of the INQUA International Commission on Sea Level Change. He is one of the world's leading ocean scientists and has specialized for thirty-five years in studying sea levels. He declared that despite normal minor fluctuations in sea level, "the sea is not rising" and that "it hasn't risen in 50 years." He claims that during the remaining decades of this century the rise in sea level will "not be more than 10 cm (4 inches), with an uncertainty of plus or minus 10 cm." The physicist explains that exaggerated AGW claims about a rise in sea level are in error because they are based solely on computer model predictions, whereas his findings are based on "going into the field to observe what is actually happening in the real world."[14]

Mörner documented his findings in a booklet, *The Greatest Lie Ever*

Told. He related that the reason the ancient city of Venice is in trouble is that the city's foundations are sinking, not that the Mediterranean Sea is rising. He also pointed out that the IPCC incorrectly published that sea levels were rising by 2.3 mm annually (one-tenth of an inch). Mörner discovered that the claimed rise in sea level was based on a single tide gauge in Hong Kong harbor, which showed a 2.3 mm rise. This increase was then extrapolated globally because (as the IPCC scientists admitted) they "needed to show a trend."[15]

It's not just islands in the Pacific that Gore claims will be submerged by rising oceans. He has stated that major cities along coastal areas will be affected. His *An Inconvenient Truth* PowerPoint presentation illustrates with maps the projected submersion of numerous areas, including the island of Manhattan, half of Florida, the Netherlands, and Bangladesh.[16] In light of the fact that there is no evidence of a significant rise in ocean levels from global warming, this prediction is nothing more than unfounded alarmism.

Scientists are researching ocean levels utilizing the Pacific Marine Atlas program, which gathers data from the entire network of automated ocean-measuring stations. They have determined that there was a significant *down-trend* in global sea levels over the past six years. Their report declared, "By using the data from the 'ARGO' global network of sea level measurements it was found that ocean levels have actually been decreasing and not rising, contrary to global warming forecasters."[17] The ARGO ocean sensory array is part of the Integrated Ocean Observing System, involving 3,198 probes that have been positioned in the oceans since November 2007. These are small, drifting robotic probes that go as deep as 2 km (1.2 mi), then surface every ten days to transmit their data to satellites. The project was set up in 2004 and is a collaboration between fifty research and operational agencies from twenty-six countries.[18]

IS THE KILIMANJARO GLACIER MELTING?

Gore claims that global warming has been melting the snows on the famous glacier on Mount Kilimanjaro in Africa.[19] However, historical records reveal that the melting of the Furtwängler Glacier on the mountain's summit began more than a century ago, around 1875.[20] When Ernest Hemingway wrote his 1936 novel *The Snows of Kilimanjaro,* significant melting had already occurred due to long-term local climate shifts. These changes were caused primarily by massive deforestation.

Gore's book claims that 40 percent of the globe's population depends on the glacial meltwaters from Himalayan glaciers for their water supply.[21] He further states that these glaciers are failing due to man-made global warming.[22] However, this false claim reflects on Gore's fundamental scientific misunderstanding of the nature of the Himalayan glaciers. The water supply derived from the Himalayan mountains is produced almost entirely from the melting of annual snowfall, not from the melting of the more permanent glacial ice. Since 1970 there has been no decline in the amount of snowmelt in Eurasia that provides the water supply to the vast population of the subcontinent.[23]

ARE THE ANTARCTIC ICE SHELVES "BREAKING UP"?

Gore says disturbing changes have been measured under the West Antarctic ice sheet, implicitly because of global warming.[24] Yet most of the recession in this ice sheet over the past ten thousand years has occurred in the absence of any rise in the sea level or any significant increase in average global temperature. In most of Antarctica, the ice is, in fact, growing thicker. The mean Antarctic temperature has actually fallen throughout the past half century.[25]

In his PowerPoint presentation, Gore claims that six massive ice shelves "larger than Rhode Island" have broken up and disappeared from the Antarctic Peninsula. Of course, he implies that this is due to global warming. While this iceberg activity is dramatic, we need to understand what global-warming alarmists never point out. Global warming is highly unlikely to have been the real cause of ice shelves breaking up. Gore does not explain that the ice shelves have melted many times, and long before the last century's rise of CO_2 in the atmosphere. The Antarctic Peninsula, where dramatic calving of icebergs takes place, accounts for only 2 percent of the ice-covered continent. Most of the Antarctic ice is growing thicker and the average temperature is cooling.[26] To gain perspective, we should remember that the cooling continent of Antarctica holds 90 percent of the ice on earth and an enormous proportion of earth's potential fresh water. The mean Antarctic temperature has grown colder throughout the past half century. Since 1978, satellites have recorded a decline every decade of 0.42°C (0.76°F).[27]

The scientific reality that you will never learn from the global-warming alarmist crowd is that the ice sheet covering most of the Antarctic continent is growing thicker every year. Further, Antarctica is not becoming warmer each year but is growing colder. Measurements of total sea ice indicate that the ice is gaining by 45 billion tons of mass annually.[28]

IS THERE DANGER OF THE GREENLAND ICE SHEET MELTING?

Greenland's ice sheet extends almost 1,600 miles from north to south and almost 700 miles east to west in the north, covering almost 660,000 square miles.[29] While Gore warns of the danger of Greenland's ice melting into the ocean, the ice sheets (up to three miles thick) rest in a bowl-like depression in bedrock created by the ice's staggering weight. With the ice resting in a huge bedrock depression, it is not going to slip into the ocean anytime soon. Gore's imaginary "dynamical ice flow" is simply impossible. The reality is that "most of Greenland lies beneath an ice cap twice the size of Australia and up to 14,000 ft (4,300 m) thick."[30]

Reports reveal that Greenland's ice is actually gaining approximately two inches of depth every year.[31] We also need to recognize that the Greenland ice sheet survived throughout the three past significantly warmer interglacial periods, when global temperatures were up to 5°C (9°F) warmer than they are today.[32]

PREDICTIONS OF COLDER WINTERS

Meteorologist Bobby Boyd, of the National Weather Service local office based in Nashville, reported on March 1, 2010, "It's been unusually cold this winter across Middle Tennessee (coldest in 30 years) with all three winter months below normal in temperature at Nashville for the first time since the winter of 1977–1978."[33] Gore's home state of Tennessee has not been cooperating with his global-warming alarmism.

Even South Florida refused to cooperate with Gore's warming predictions. The National Weather Service's Weather Forecast Office reported, "A colder-than-normal February wrapped up the coldest winter since the early 1980s over south Florida. Almost all main weather reporting sites recorded the coldest December–February average temperature since 1981."[34]

One writer in the UK noted, "Temperatures in December, January and February struggled to stay above zero, with the UK's average a chilly 1.5c (35f), making it the deepest freeze since 1978-79.... The Met Office has confirmed that 2009/10 winter was the coldest since 1978/79.... And in Scotland and Northern Ireland it was the coldest winter since 1962-63."[35]

In an extensive opinion that appeared in 2010 in the *New York Times,* Gore stated, "I, for one, genuinely wish that the climate crisis were an illusion."[36]

In light of the former vice president's frantic doomsday pronouncements—and the fact that he is earning untold millions of dollars annually through his carbon-credit business and his books, videos, and presentations—I admit I remain just a little skeptical about the sincerity of his claim.

INSURANCE LOSSES INCREASE DUE TO GLOBAL WARMING

An Inconvenient Truth implies that massive insurance losses are being produced as a result of large hurricanes, tropical storms, and other extreme weather events that are increasing due to global warming.[37] Here are the facts. Insured losses were lower in 2005 (the year of Hurricane Katrina) than they were in 1925, when calculated as a percentage of the population of coastal areas at risk. The real reason for the massive increase in hurricane insurance claim losses in recent years is that people are increasingly building high-value residential and industrial properties on vulnerable coastline areas.[38]

While Gore claims that many scientists are warning that hurricanes will become stronger due to global warming,[39] there is no scientific support for this statement.[40]

In a similar vein, *An Inconvenient Truth* claims severe tornadoes are increasing due to global warming.[41] However, the number of severe tornadoes has been dropping during the last five decades.[42] The increase in the overall number of tornado reports is due to the greatly increased accuracy of meteorological detection systems, which can detect many smaller tornadoes that would previously not have been reported.[43]

WHAT IS GORE'S SCIENTIFIC EXPERTISE?

Gore's *An Inconvenient Truth* suggests that an increase of only 100 parts per million by volume (ppmv) of CO_2 in the atmosphere (a rise from 385 ppmv to 485 ppm) would produce the difference between an ice-age temperature minimum and an interglacial temperature maximum. He claims this increase in CO_2 could cause "the difference between a nice day and having a mile of ice above your head."[44] This is simply not true. Gore overstates by ten times the mainstream climate science consensus estimate of the effect of rising levels of CO_2 on global temperature.[45]

Further, Gore refers in his speeches to carbon dioxide as "global warming pollution." Unfortunately, the U.S. Environmental Protection Agency (EPA) has officially declared that CO_2 is a pollutant that should be regulated by the federal government. However, CO_2 is not a pollutant; it is a vital atmospheric trace gas that is an essential nutrient and food for plant life. Without CO_2, there would be no plant life and therefore no animal life on earth.

Far from being harmful, geological science has revealed that even at CO_2 concentrations twenty times higher than at the present time (up to 7,000 ppmv), even the most delicate plants would grow much more quickly.[46] As carbon dioxide increases gradually over the following decades due to our continued use of fossil fuels, this rise in atmospheric levels of CO_2 will accelerate the growth rate of many plants that are essential to feed the world's growing population. Many greenhouses maintain a level of CO_2 in the air three times higher than the normal atmosphere to accelerate plant growth.

The contradictions and errors of fact pointed out in this chapter lead to one conclusion: Al Gore does not have a background or demonstrated expertise in climate science. During a November 12, 2009, interview on *The Tonight Show,* he promoted a number of renewable energy sources that he suggested might soon provide an alternative to fossil fuels. Speaking of the tremendous energy potential that could be provided by inexhaustible amounts of geothermal energy, Gore claimed that the temperature in the interior of the earth is "several million degrees."

"People think about geothermal energy—when they think about it at all—in terms of the hot water bubbling up in some places. But two kilometers or so down in most places there are these incredibly hot rocks, 'cause the interior of the earth is extremely hot, several million degrees, and the crust of the earth is hot," he stated.[47] In truth, if the temperature of the earth's interior were "several million degrees," the earth would be a star and we would not be able to live on the planet. Although we have not penetrated the earth's crust more than nine miles, the majority of scientists agree that the temperature several miles down in the earth's crust will not reach more than 2,000 degrees.

For more than a century, geologists have measured the temperature deep in the earth using sensitive thermometers lowered into boreholes in coal mines and gold mines. The temperature of the earth's core is estimated to be approximately 9,000°F. The Savuka Mine is the deepest mine in the world at two miles. The deepest borehole used by geologists reached a maximum of less than 9.4 miles. When the temperature in the earth's crust exceeds 2,000°F, rocks begin to melt. So Gore's "several million degrees" was wrong by at least a factor of one thousand, or 100,000 percent.

The universal use of geothermal energy is not realizable at this time because the earth's geothermal temperatures are not high enough in most locations to make extracting heat energy practical. At this point the useful development of dependable geothermal energy is limited to unusual geological areas such as the island of Iceland, which is located in a geological anomaly with continuous volcanic activity. Gore told Conan O'Brien's television audience that the known U.S. geothermal resources are so enormous they could provide all the energy America needs for the next 35,000 years.[48] However, the reality is that less than 1 percent of America's energy is derived from geothermal sources.

Gore went on to claim that we can work effectively with geothermal energy because we now have "new drill bits that don't melt in that heat."[49] How is it possible that anyone with this level of scientific ignorance can present himself to the world as the climate-science guru? How can the news media, normally skeptical about extreme claims, be so accepting of Gore's arguments that he says "prove" man-made global warming? How can anyone take Gore seriously, whether on the basis of scientific claims or in his climate-change recommendations?

Climategate: Hiding the Flaws in Global-Warming Data

An unnamed climate scientist is credited with the unauthorized release of more than four thousand private e-mails and climate-data files. Posted on the Internet on November 20, 2009, the e-mails and files originated from the Climate Research Unit (CRU) at the University of East Anglia in the United Kingdom—one of three key climate research centers.[1] With the release of revealing (and highly embarrassing) internal documents, the anthropogenic global-warming (AGW) juggernaut came to a temporary halt.

This game-changing event is known as Climategate. I expect that someday the unknown scientist at CRU will be known as a hero who risked his or her career to allow the public and other scientists to examine the research data on their own. Those of us who suspected that the temperature records had been "cooked" to support a predetermined global-warming conclusion were finally able to look at the data and expose the climate scientists' hidden agenda.

The sharing of original data among scientists is vital for the progress of scientific research, especially in a field that is fraught with controversy and massive economic as well as political policy implications. The UK government determined that some of the leading scientists at the CRU had broken the law by refusing to release the data they possessed on historical temperature levels. They were legally obligated to release this data to other scientists as a result of the filing of more than ninety-five Freedom of Information Act requests.[2]

Under the requirements of the UK's Freedom of Information Act, any tax-supported institution must promptly comply with any legitimate request from other accredited scientists to share original research data. This allows other scientists to check and verify an institution's announced scientific conclusions.

Attempts to deny climate skeptics their legal and academic rights to review another scientist's data strongly suggest bias and paranoia on the part of the CRU scientists. The reluctance to share their research data also causes growing suspicion that climate scientists who advance the theory of AGW have something to hide.[3]

SCIENTISTS FALSIFY DATA BY DENYING A PAST PERIOD OF WARMING

In 2001, then University of Virginia professor Michael Mann, a climate scientist specializing in historical temperature data, introduced his infamous "hockey-stick graph." He claimed that the graph demonstrates that human activities involving the use of fossil fuels are producing runaway global warming. His historical-scientific analysis of climate data was derived from recorded temperature readings during the last one and a half centuries, plus historical temperature projections derived from temperature "proxies," including tree rings, Arctic and Antarctic ice core drillings, and deep seabed sediments. (Because temperature records were not kept before 1860, these proxies are the next best thing.)

Reading the e-mails that were leaked during Climategate, it becomes clear that leading AGW alarmist scientists, such as Mann and Phil Jones at the CRU, seemed obsessed with discrediting their leading critics. Stephen McIntyre, a retired mining engineer, and Dr. Ross McKitrick, professor of economics at the University of Guelph (Canada), were two of the leading scholars who analyzed the data and questioned the conclusions.

Mann and others graphed what they said was an accurate record of the historic temperature data. However, they manipulated the data by artificially eliminating both the Medieval Warm Period and the Little Ice Age—two centuries-long periods of massive temperature variation that occurred long before significant CO_2 emissions by humans. It is complicated work to analyze, but it's the sort of statistical analysis that McIntyre and McKitrick are used to performing. For example, as a mining engineer, McIntyre would study sets of core samples in an attempt to draw sound conclusions about the likely location and extent of mineral deposits. McIntyre and McKitrick closely examined how Mann and others had produced their mathematical work. The two analysts determined that Mann and others had manipulated the data in order to support a predetermined conclusion. McIntyre and McKitrick published their work discrediting Mann's graph in the journal *Energy and Environment*.[4]

When McIntyre and McKitrick published their first devastating hockey-stick-graph analysis in 2003, Mann sent an angry e-mail to his colleagues, telling them how to deal with "M & M." "The important thing is to deny that this has any intellectual credibility whatsoever and, if contacted by any media, to dismiss this for the stunt that it is."[5]

Raymond Bradley, a climatologist with the University of Massachusetts at Amherst and part of the Intergovernmental Panel on Climate Change (IPCC), suggested that CRU should provide the "independent" voice that would discredit McIntyre and McKitrick. "If an 'independent group' such as you guys at CRU could make a statement as to whether the M & M effort is truly an 'audit,' and if they did it right, I think that would go a long way to defusing the issue.… If you are willing, a quick and forceful statement from The Distinguished CRU Boys would help quash further arguments."[6]

When confronted by statistical scientists who disproved the "flat" temperature record during the last millennium, which is shown in the "hockey-stick" graph, Mann and his global-warming colleagues denied that they falsified any of the temperature statistics. They later claimed that they merely "normalized" the earlier raw temperature data.[7]

University of Oklahoma geology professor Dr. David Deming claimed that he received an e-mail from someone deeply involved in the AGW movement. The e-mail read, "We have to get rid of the Medieval Warm Period."[8] And that is what happened when the IPCC replaced an earlier graph used in its 1990 global-warming report with the new hockey-stick graph in 2001.

The graph developed by Mann, author of eighty academic publications, indicates that the climate in the Northern Hemisphere remained basically unchanged for almost a thousand years. Following that long stable period, the temperature rose rapidly in the last century as a result of the increase of carbon dioxide in the atmosphere due to industrial activity, electrical power production using fossil fuels, and widespread use of gasoline- and diesel-powered modes of transportation.

The graph also enhanced by at least 50 percent the actual temperature increase that occurred since 1980 in an attempt to suggest that the rise of

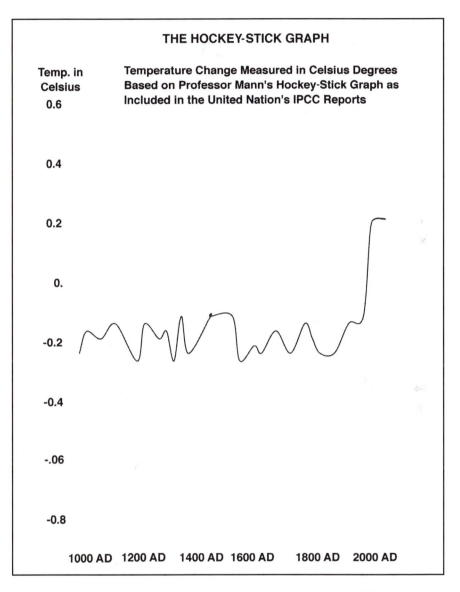

THE HOCKEY-STICK GRAPH

Temp. in Celsius
0.6

Temperature Change Measured in Celsius Degrees
Based on Professor Mann's Hockey-Stick Graph as
Included in the United Nation's IPCC Reports

0.4

0.2

0.

-0.2

-0.4

-.06

-0.8

1000 AD   1200 AD   1400 AD   1600 AD   1800 AD   2000 AD

global temperatures in recent centuries was unprecedented. The graph re-
sembles a hockey stick lying in a horizontal position with the blade at the end
rising diagonally (representing the recent increase in global temperature.)
This graph appears six times in the IPCC's 2001 assessment report, and in
full color.

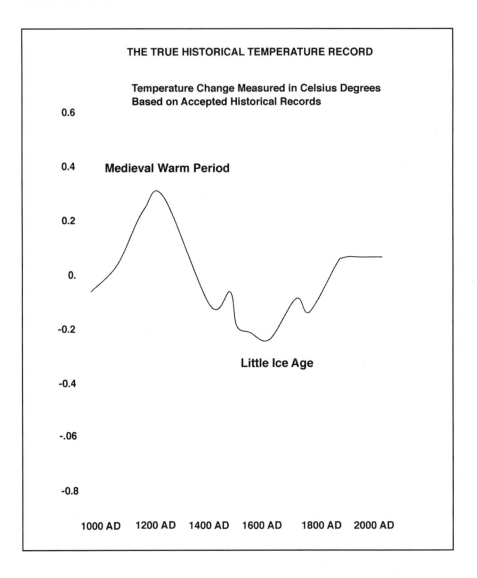

THE TRUE HISTORICAL TEMPERATURE RECORD

Temperature Change Measured in Celsius Degrees
Based on Accepted Historical Records

Medieval Warm Period

Little Ice Age

The hockey-stick graph and its dismissal of major temperature variations during the Medieval Warm Period and the Little Ice Age has been the target of criticism within the scientific community. In response, the AGW movement has marshaled its forces to defend the biased "science" that legitimizes the false theory of man-made global warming.

REVELATIONS REGARDING GLOBAL-WARMING FRAUD

In the late fall of 2009, someone with access to the Climate Research Unit (CRU) files and e-mails gathered more than a thousand e-mails exchanged by leading global-warming scientists, as well as more than three thousand scientific data files. The person posted the e-mails and files on the Internet, so that outsiders who accessed the material could see the manipulations of historical temperature data. The files and e-mails show that IPCC-affiliated scientists went to great lengths to hide their data for more than a decade to prevent review by other climate scientists.

CRU scientists, led by Professor Phil Jones, did everything possible to deny legitimate outside requests to examine their data. An indication of this is seen in an e-mail sent from Jones to Mann, creator of the hockey-stick graph.

Mike,

...Just sent loads of station data to Scott. Make sure he documents everything better this time ! And don't leave stuff lying around on ftp sites [File Transfer Protocol]—you never know who is trawling them. The two MMs [Canadian scientists Ross McKitrick and Steve McIntyre, who exposed Mann's statistical errors in his hockey-stick graph] have been after the CRU station data for years. If they ever hear there is a Freedom of Information Act now in the UK, I think I'll delete the file rather than send to anyone. Does your similar act in the US force you to respond to enquiries within 20 days?—our[s] does! The UK works on precedents, so the first request will test it.

We also have a data protection act, which I will hide behind. Tom Wigley has sent me a worried email when he heard about it—thought people could ask him for his model code. He has retired officially from UEA [University of East Anglia] so he can hide behind that. IPR [Intellectual Property Rights] should be relevant here.[9]

The scientists who were exchanging such e-mails were a small but enormously influential group. Approximately three dozen UK and American scientists are the most influential group of climate scientists in the world. They supplied the "scientific authority" supporting the United Nations–promoted panic and fear over the looming threat of man-made global warming. They also exercise overwhelming influence over the writing of the IPCC's Summary Reports.

Jones controlled the presentation of two sets of historical climate temperature data that were used by the IPCC to draw up its major environmental reports. Jones's records are the most important of the four sets of historical temperature data that form a basis for the IPCC's policy recommendations to national governments. Those recommendations include far-reaching and intrusive changes in national energy and economic policies, carbon taxes, and cap-and-trade policies that propose reducing man-made carbon dioxide contributions to the atmosphere.

The CRU selects virtually every one of the IPCC's key scientific contributors. That means Jones was in a position to influence the scientists who compiled data for the United Nations' climate reports, which exaggerated temperature records during the last century. The modified records supported the AGW movement's political position that humanity must abandon the use of fossil fuels and the prosperous, affluent lifestyle and economic systems made possible by cheap energy. History reveals that the ready availability of inexpensive and reliable fossil-fuel energy transformed the lives of the citizens of Europe and North America, and later within the liberated nations of Eastern Europe and Russia, and even China. Many supporters of AGW admit they want to prevent similar economic transformations from taking place in the developing nations of Africa, South America, and south Asia.

The globalist elites plan to drastically reduce the standard of living in the West for their own political purposes. They also want to prevent the Third World from benefiting from Western technology, which would improve their economies and the quality of life of their citizens.

SENATOR INHOFE'S LONGSTANDING OPPOSITION TO AGW

U.S. Senator Jim Inhofe, the ranking Republican member of the Senate Committee on Environment and Public Works, is a serious opponent of the AGW movement. In 2010 Inhofe made public a preview of a Senate minority report on his committee's investigation into Climategate. The report is titled "'Consensus' Exposed: The CRU Controversy."

The committee report provides incontrovertible evidence that the CRU e-mails released in the fall of 2009 show the world's leading climate scientists

- discussing ways to obstruct the release of data and information that is damaging to the man-made global-warming cause and movement;

- discussing the manipulation of research data to support predetermined conclusions;

- threatening journal editors who publish work questioning the climate-science "consensus";

- assuming activist roles to influence the political process, rather than being committed to pure scientific research—no matter what conclusions it leads to.[10]

The committee examined the four-thousand-plus e-mails and data files produced by the CRU at East Anglia over a thirteen-year period, between 1996 and November 2009. The CRU e-mails reveal that the supposed consensus on man-made global warming is a manufactured illusion. Despite the movement's repeated assertions that the "science is settled," the released e-mails reveal that leading climate scientists continue to argue over critical issues and raise questions regarding key analysis methods and statistical techniques. Most astonishing, the CRU e-mails reveal key scientists who doubt whether there is a consensus regarding the causes and extent of climate change.

The Senate minority report on Climategate issues demands that the federal government reevaluate the entire AGW issue, along with a review of government tax and regulation plans that are based on faulty scientific evidence. The report claimed, "It's time for the Obama Administration to recognize this. Its endangerment finding for greenhouse gases rests on bad science. It should throw out that finding and abandon greenhouse gas regulation under the Clean Air Act—a policy that will mean fewer jobs, higher taxes and economic decline."[11]

THE FALLOUT FROM CLIMATEGATE

In the early months of 2010, following the unauthorized release on the Internet of thousands of secret data files and up to 1,032 e-mail messages from the CRU of the University of East Anglia (UK), confidence wavered among major public supporters of global-warming science. It was widely reported that a key IPCC leader (Phil Jones of the CRU) admitted in 2010 for the first time that there has been no "statistically significant" rise in global temperature for the last fifteen years.[12]

Stephen Schneider, Stanford professor of climatology and lead author of many IPCC reports, suggested that scientists should exaggerate their level of confidence in the probability of man-made global warming in order to motivate voters and political leaders to act, regardless of any remaining doubts.

On the one hand, as scientists we are ethically bound to the scientific method, in effect promising to tell the truth, the whole truth, and nothing but—which means that we must include all the doubts, the caveats, the ifs, ands, and buts. On the other hand, we are not just scientists but human beings as well. And like most people would like to see the world a better place, which in this context translates into our working to reduce the risk of potentially disastrous climatic change. To do that we need to get some broad based support, to capture the public's imagination.... So we have to offer up scary scenarios, make simplified, dramatic statements and make little mention of any doubts.... Each of us has to decide what the right balance is between being effective and being honest. I hope that means being both.[13]

Climate scientists plan a cover-up

It is instructive to consider several of the thousand-plus CRU e-mails that were released in November 2009. On May 29, 2008, Jones sent the following request to Mann, creator of the infamous hockey-stick temperature graph. Jones's e-mail reads,

> Mike,
>
> Can you delete any emails you may have had with Keith re AR4? Keith will do likewise....
>
> Can you also email Gene and get him to do the same? I don't have his new email address.
>
> We will be getting Caspar to do likewise.
>
> Cheers, Phil[14]

AR4 refers to the IPCC's Fourth Assessment Report, published by the United Nations in 2007, to summarize for political leaders and the news media the climate-science research supporting the theory of man-made global warming. The report was designed to educate and motivate political leaders to formulate government policies to reduce greenhouse gases. It is difficult to reach any conclusion other than to assume Jones wanted leading climate scientists to destroy their e-mail communications that revealed their influence on the United Nations' most vital climate-change document, AR4. Further, the e-mail communication between Jones and the other scientists occurred at the same time ninety-five Freedom of Information requests were filed, seeking access to the CRU's data files.

An e-mail with the subject line "reconstruction errors," sent from Mann to Professor Tim Osborn, refers to past unusually warm periods, especially during the centuries known as the Medieval Warm Period (900–1300). Mann acknowledges periods of warmer global temperatures centuries before the level of CO_2 in the atmosphere rose. He concludes with this revealing and cautionary statement to his colleague: "p.s. I know I probably don't need to mention this, but just to insure absolutely clarify [sic] on this, I'm providing these for your own personal use, since you're a trusted colleague. So please don't pass this along to others without checking w/ me first. This is the sort of 'dirty laundry' one doesn't want to fall into the hands of those who might potentially try to distort things."[15]

In another communication sent from the CRU, Dr. Tom Wigley explains to Jones their reasons for refusing to send requested data to outside scientists, despite the Freedom of Information legal requirements. "The issue of with-holding [sic] data is still a hot potato, one that affects both you and Keith (and Mann). Yes, there are reasons—but many *good* scientists appear to be unsympathetic to these. The trouble here is that with-holding [sic] data looks like hiding something, and hiding means (in some eyes) that it is bogus science that is being hidden."[16]

MAIN CONCERNS ARISING FROM CLIMATEGATE

Three significant issues present themselves as primary areas of concern. The first is the CRU scientists' habit of concealing data, even when formal requests for access had been made by outside scientists. Second is the deliberate alteration of historical temperature records. And third is the practice of pressuring and silencing critics of the AGW theory.

The first concern: hiding data

The CRU e-mails reveal a widespread and long-term campaign to prevent the release of their original historical temperature data to other climate scientists. Under the Freedom of Information Act of the United Kingdom, any tax-supported institution must respond expeditiously to any request to release scientific data to a recognized scientific colleague. Jones and his fellow scientists in the UK and the United States refused to release requested data for many years. But why were they so determined to hide their temperature data?

Here is one explanation: These taxpayer-supported climate-research institutions have presented scientific conclusions that endorse massive societal, political, and economic changes. But the rationale for these changes is based on historical temperature data that has been hidden from peer review. It also appears that historical temperature data was manipulated in order to achieve computer models that generated the desired results, "proving" that increased CO_2 in the atmosphere causes higher global temperatures.[17]

According to an IPCC report, there was a warming of 0.6°+/– 0.2°C during the twentieth century. Australian climate scientist Warwick Hughes was naturally curious about the source and explanation of the variation of "+/– 0.2°C" and where it originated. Hughes wrote to Jones in 2005 and requested, as a fellow researcher, the original temperature data. Jones's response to Hughes, who was simply attempting to replicate Jones's climate research, was remarkable but also quite revealing. "We have 25 years or so invested in the work. Why should I make the data available to you, when your aim is to try and find something wrong with it?"[18]

More recently, Professor Jones has astonishingly claimed that much of his original temperature data has been lost. This begs the question: what is it about the underlying historical temperature data that CRU scientists are so desperate to hide?

"The academic [Phil Jones] at the centre of the 'Climategate' affair, whose raw data is crucial to the theory of climate change, has admitted that he has trouble 'keeping track' of the information. Colleagues say that the reason Professor Phil Jones has refused Freedom of Information requests is that he may have actually lost the relevant papers."[19]

Now we can understand the meaning of Jones's e-mail message to Mann, quoted earlier: "From Phil Jones. To: Michael Mann. Date: May 29, 2008: 'Can you delete any emails you may have had with Keith re AR4 [the IPCC Fourth Assessment Report]? Keith will do likewise.'"

The second concern: altering historical temperature data

CRU climate scientists chose to falsify historical temperature data through manipulation of computer formulas and climate-model programs. By adjusting temperature records in order to minimize the temperatures during warmer periods in the past, they could suggest that the climate in recent decades reflects an unprecedented period of significantly rising temperatures. Thus they "documented" a unique, accelerated global-warming pattern that endangers life on earth.

McIntyre examined both Mann's underlying data (supporting the hockey-stick graph) and Dr. James Hansen's Goddard Institute for Space Studies (GISS) temperature records, derived from ground-temperature measuring sites. McIntyre demonstrated that both of the scientists' global-warming data and conclusions were unsupported by the actual underlying temperature data.[20]

In America, Australia, and New Zealand, independent researchers have demonstrated that many of the historical temperature-data claims made by man-made global-warming alarmists are unsupported by original historical temperature records. The degree of manipulation of historical temperature data was extraordinary. Climate records were systematically manipulated so that periods of unusually warm weather, such as the 1930s, were minimized or even eliminated. Meanwhile, the very gradual warming that occurred (1.3°F) since 1860 was exaggerated to make it appear that it was unprecedented in history, and therefore probably caused by the rise of atmospheric carbon dioxide.[21]

The third issue: silencing critics

CRU e-mails that were posted on the Internet show the methods climate scientists used to defame and silence skeptics who dared to question AGW conclusions. The e-mails reveal that these scientists not only denied requests to disclose data, but they actively discredited and refused to work with any scientific journal that dared to publish any of their critics' articles.[22]

A small but influential group of about three dozen climate scientists at the UK's CRU, at the Goddard Institute for Space Studies (GISS), and at Pennsylvania State University did everything possible to stifle any genuine public scientific debate regarding climate change. They also used their influence to make certain that no dissenting research could be published as part of the UN's IPCC reports.[23]

In 2006, mathematician Dr. Edward Wegman presented a report to Congress that confirmed the accuracy of McIntyre's statistical repudiation of Mann's hockey-stick graph that hid major climate changes in the past millennium including the Medieval Warm Period. Wegman's report revealed that Mann purposely hid evidence of the Medieval Warm Period and the Little

Ice Age to create the illusion that the earth's climate had experienced no pre-vious significant warming period prior to the Industrial Revolution. Weg-man condemned the manner in which these elite climate scientists collabo-rate and support one another's conclusions and reports. The AGW climate scientists arrange to validate their fellow scientists' papers. As a result, a small group of global-warming-supporting scientists have been able to dominate the reports included in IPCC reports.

As a result of the Climategate crisis, Dr. Phil Jones, former head of the CRU at the University of East Anglia, was forced to resign. However, CRU scien-tists who had refused to comply with ninety-five Freedom of Information requests for research data were absolved of any crime. The investigations also absolved them of any legal responsibility for deleting requested climate data. (The UK investigations were led by individuals who were openly declared supporters of the AGW position.)

Jones was later allowed to resume his previous position as head of the Cli-mate Research Unit. He recently admitted that despite the continued growth in man-made carbon dioxide contributions to the atmosphere, *"For the past 15 years [1995–2010] there has been no 'statistically significant' warming."*[24]

Professor Jones's admission reveals that those who have been the declared champions of AGW are now faced with undeniable evidence that totally re-pudiates their decades of confident predictions of rising levels of global warm-ing that is caused by continued additions of man-made emissions of carbon dioxide to the atmosphere.

Fundamentally, the reality of twelve years of global cooling since 1998, in spite of the continued growth of CO_2 in the air from human production of emissions, repudiates their theory of man-made global warming.

The Truth About Temperature Change

T he basic argument behind anthropogenic global warming (AGW) is based not on observable, measured evidence of higher temperature readings, but rather on computer-model predictions and potential scenarios of possible future climate change. The computer models make global climate predictions based on extremely complex formulae and arbitrarily chosen data inputs. Astonishingly, the climate-change models either do not include or greatly minimize the impact of cloud formations, solar radiation cycles, volcanic eruptions, and the massive climate effects of El Niño or La Niña.[1]

The sun is the greatest single contributing factor to the earth's climate. And although climate scientists and meteorologists are aware that cloud cover and solar radiation significantly influence the climate in profound ways, they are not yet able to accurately measure these influences. Nor can they accurately account for the impact of clouds and the sun in the computer models they use to predict future global warming

Every single one of the dozens of computer climate models used by the United Nations Intergovernmental Panel on Climate Change (IPCC) failed to predict that the earth's climate would significantly cool after 1997 and that the climate would continue to cool for the following twelve years. Note that this cooling trend took place during a time when humanity continued to produce enormous amounts of carbon dioxide, which was added to the atmosphere. How can anyone believe the AGW alarmist predictions of massive global warming during the coming century when the IPCC climate models totally failed to predict that the global temperature would stop rising in 1997 and that a gradual cooling trend would begin that has lasted twelve years to date (2010)?

THE SUN AND GLOBAL TEMPERATURES

A review of temperature patterns since 1860 reveals a close correlation between temperature averages and solar activity. A comparison of the historical pattern of sunspot cycles closely correlates with the rise and fall of global temperatures. Every *second*, the sun sends to earth an amount of energy that equals the energy released by a devastating earthquake (magnitude 8 on the Richter scale). It has been calculated that the amount of solar energy sent to earth in just one hour is equal to all the energy expended by humanity during an entire year.[2]

Scientists who study solar radiation are generally skeptical that the increase in carbon dioxide in the atmosphere during the last half century produced the global warming of 1°F since 1900. Recently, solar scientists from the United Kingdom, Germany, and South Korea concluded that the recent drop in sunspot activity (indicating a lessening of the intensity of solar radiation) was linked to the unusually cold weather that Europe has experienced since 1998.[3]

The recent period of low sunspot activity could lead to a series of very cold winters.[4] This cooler period could prove similar to weather patterns that occurred during the Little Ice Age in the 1600s, when sunspot activity was at an extreme minimum. The study discovered that low solar radiation activity (accompanied by minimum sunspots) corresponded closely with periods of excessively cold winters. This correlation has been validated for centuries. Professor Mike Lockwood of the University of Reading, the lead author of the solar radiation–climate study, concluded, "There is less than a 1% probability that the result was obtained by chance."[5] In other words, it is 99 percent likely that the low sunspot activity reveals low solar-radiation activity, which historically produces colder global temperatures and colder winters.

Professor Henrik Svensmark, of the Danish National Space Institute, concluded that IPCC reports were "probably totally wrong" in dismissing without consideration the contribution of the sun to the earth's climate.[6]

Most solar scientists conclude that the cause-and-effect relationship between variations in solar cycles and subsequent changes in the earth's climate is incontrovertible. Solar scientists increasingly believe that the burden of scientific evidence supports the view that the Roman Warm Period (250 BC–AD 450) and the Medieval Warm Period (AD 900–1300) were significantly warmer than our current climate. Obviously, these warmer periods occurred long before humanity's significant production of carbon dioxide. The significantly warmer periods in past eras were caused by the solar activity, not by humanity's contributions of CO_2 to the atmosphere.

In March 2010 the Saskatchewan Isotope Laboratory at the University of Saskatchewan, together with the University of Colorado's Institute of Arctic and Alpine Research, published a fascinating study in the *Proceedings of the National Academy of Sciences of the United States of America*. The study documented for the first time scientific evidence of seasonal temperature variations in the North Atlantic Ocean covering the last two millennia, from 360 BC till AD 1660. Their study confirmed seasonal temperature variations during two thousand years through the precise measurement of oxygen and carbon isotopes captured in mollusk shells in the ocean seabed. The study confirmed that the Roman Warm Period in the centuries around the time of Christ was the warmest period in the last two thousand years. The study declared, "The interval from 230 B.C. to A.D. 40 was one of exceptional warmth in Iceland, coinciding with a period of general warmth and dryness in Europe known as the Roman Warm Period, from 200 B.C. to A.D. 400. On the basis of ^{18}O [an isotope of oxygen] data, reconstructed water temperatures for the Roman Warm Period in Iceland are higher than any temperatures recorded in modern times."[7]

Research scientist Professor Nicola Scafetta and Duke University physics professor Bruce West published their solar climate research in 2005 in the research journal *Geophysical Research Letters*. After extensive evaluation of precise satellite sensor readings of global temperature since 1979, they concluded, "At least 10 to 30 percent of global warming measured during the past two decades may be due to increased solar output rather than factors such as increased heat-absorbing carbon dioxide gas released by various human activities."[8]

In 2008, Dr. West criticized the IPCC for having "concluded that the contribution of solar variability to global warming is negligible."[9] He noted that the majority of global-warming researchers and their computer models have not adequately allowed for the impact of the sun's radiation on earth's climate.

Scafetta and West produced a report in 2006 in which they concluded, "We estimate that the sun contributed as much as 45–50% of the 1900–2000 global warming, and 25–35% of the 1980–2000 global warming.

These results, while confirming that anthropogenic-added climate forcing might have progressively played a dominant role in climate change during the last century, also suggest that the solar impact on climate change during the same period is significantly stronger than what some theoretical models have predicted."[10] Scafetta and West reached these conclusions by applying a mathematical formula that closely compares the variations in solar cycles to the variations in global temperature cycles.

NASA's Mars Global Surveyor and Odyssey missions revealed that the carbon dioxide icecap at Mars's south pole has significantly diminished during the previous three summers. Professor Habibullo Abdussamatov is the leader of space research at St. Petersburg's Pulkovo Astronomical Observatory in Russia. Professor Abdussamatov declared that the Mars data provides irrefutable evidence that the long-term global warming during the last century on earth, very similar to that which is occurring on Mars, is caused by changes in solar radiation. According to Abdussamatov, "The long-term increase in solar irradiance is heating both Earth and Mars."[11]

Unless Martians have recently industrialized their planet and are producing massive quantities of atmospheric carbon dioxide, the only reasonable scientific conclusion is that the very gradual global warming demonstrated on both planets must be caused by the one factor affecting both planets—the sun's radiation.

Meanwhile, astronomers discovered that the red planet increased its average temperature by 0.65°C (1.17°F) between the 1970s and the 1990s, almost precisely matching the gradual warming trend measured on earth during the same period.[12] This warming trend has also been detected on Jupiter,[13] Pluto, and Neptune's moon Triton. Obviously, man-made contributions of carbon dioxide on earth can't affect similar warming occurring on other bodies in the solar system.

While the global temperature gradually increased by 1°F during the last century, virtually half of that increase (0.5°F) occurred during the first half of the century at a time when humanity's production of carbon dioxide was still relatively minor. This fact strongly suggests that other climate factors are the major driving engines of the minor rise of global temperature in the last portion of the last century. Further, since 1998 the earth has been gradually cooling down to the point that almost all of the global warming (1°F) we experienced during the last century has now been erased. In contradiction of the global-warming alarmists, as humanity continues to add massive amounts of carbon dioxide to the atmosphere, the global temperature continued to cool. Significantly, this cooling trend is occurring at the same time the sun is going through a cycle that is characterized by a significant drop in solar radiation.

There is no question that greenhouse gases, including carbon dioxide and methane, play some role in moderating our climate. But the sun, as the major energy engine of the solar system, is far and away the most significant driver of earth's climate.

SUNSPOTS, CLOUDS, AND CLIMATE CHANGE

The years between 1645 and 1715 were a period with virtually no sunspot activity. It became known as the Maunder Minimum (or the "prolonged sunspot minimum"), when "frost fairs" were celebrated on the frozen River Thames in London.[14] The period is named after the astronomer Edward W. Maunder (1851–1928), who studied sunspot activity. During one thirty-year stretch, sunspot activity dropped to approximately fifty sunspots annually—compared to the historical annual average of up to *fifty thousand*. This period of extremely low sunspot activity coincided with the coldest portion of the Little Ice Age, when North America, Russia, and Europe all experienced disastrous agricultural conditions and bitterly cold winters.

Once again, we are experiencing a period of extremely low sunspot activity. The years 2008 and 2009 experienced record low numbers, with 266 (73 percent) sunspot-free days in 2008 and 260 (71 percent) days without sunspots in 2009.[15] Since the scientific evidence reveals that the cause of the mild (1°F) global warming is mostly natural solar activity opposed to man-made, there is nothing we can do about it. Obviously we can't control solar radiation or cloud cover.

Dr. G. LeBlanc Smith specialized for years in geosciences and sedimentology as the principal research scientist at Australia's Commonwealth Scientific and Industrial Research Organisation (CSIRO). Professor Smith rejected the theories of man-made global warming alarmism several years ago.

> I have yet to see credible proof of carbon dioxide driving climate change, yet [sic] alone manmade CO_2 driving it. The atmospheric hot-spot [in the troposphere] is missing and the ice core data refute this.... I contend that those professional scientists and advisors that are knowingly complicit in climate science fraud and all that is derived from it, will continue to be exposed by the science itself.... There is no atmospheric hot-spot from "greenhouse CO_2," despite over 20 years of serious looking for it. Occam's razor would point to the sun as the driver of climate change of significance. *Human generated carbon dioxide is arguably around 3% of the total carbon dioxide budget, and in the light of the above, we are effectively irrelevant to the natural climate change continuum.*[16]

How clouds influence climate

While the impact of clouds on our climate has been obvious to most people, the creators of the climate computer models chose to ignore the effect of solar radiation, the impact of water vapor (which forms 95 percent of earth's greenhouse gases), and the obvious influence of clouds. The decision to eliminate these key factors in the evaluation of climate change suggests a significant bias.

It is probable that the fact that we cannot modify or influence any of these factors (solar radiation, water vapor, or clouds) is what motivated global-warming alarmists to make CO_2 their sole focus.

Australian geologist and science author Ian Plimer has pointed out some of the severe limitations of the computer models used in creating the IPCC climate-change reports. Plimer wrote in his insightful book *Heaven and Earth* about the significant part played by cloud cover in impacting global temperatures. "The clouds in earth's atmosphere reflect some 60 percent of the sun's radiation. A change of just 1% in cloudiness of planet Earth could account for all of the 20th Century warming. However, IPCC computers don't do clouds."[17]

THE HUMAN CONTRIBUTION TO CO_2 IN THE ATMOSPHERE

Over long periods of geological and historical time, there is no evidence to support a close causal relationship between carbon dioxide levels in the air and global temperature levels. Not only is there no clearly documented cause-and-effect relationship, but human activities contribute only a tiny fraction of the CO_2 that is found in the atmosphere. Even today, all of the industrial, agricultural, and transportation activities of the human population contribute only about 3.4 percent annually to increased CO_2 levels. This is dwarfed by the 96.6 percent that is created by natural nonhuman processes. If there were no humans on the planet, or if humanity reduced its economic activities to Stone Age levels, the impact on global temperature would be so small it could scarcely be measured.

We have all heard the dire warnings about massive loss of species due to greenhouse gases and resulting global warming. However, we need to remember that scientists researching the Cambrian period found evidence of a staggering number of species of life flourishing at a time when CO_2 levels in the atmosphere were twenty-five times *higher* than today.[18] During the Jurassic period, dinosaurs prospered when CO_2 levels were nine times higher than we experience in this century.[19]

Studies involving ice-core drilling in Antarctica and Greenland demonstrate that a rise in carbon dioxide levels in the atmosphere *follows* the rise of global temperature by several centuries. A careful scientific analysis of ice-core records over 650,000 years demonstrates that global temperature increases have *preceded* rather than followed increases in CO_2.[20]

Let me repeat that. Rising levels of carbon dioxide *follow* higher global temperatures. The oceans, which cover 70 percent of the earth's surface, contain more than fifty times the amount of carbon dioxide that exists in the atmosphere. There is a constant interchange between the oceans and the atmosphere of CO_2 (approximately every five years). Carbon dioxide is more soluble in cold water than in warmer water. When the oceans warm, the water releases much more carbon dioxide into the atmosphere. However, when the oceans cool, they absorb and retain much more carbon dioxide. For a comparison, bear in mind that a warm carbonated beverage has more fizz than a cold one. It turns out that global temperature actually determines and controls the level of carbon dioxide in the atmosphere, and not the other way around.[21]

Minuscule CO_2 levels in the atmosphere

For decades, global-warming alarmists have convinced the public that increased levels of carbon dioxide in the atmosphere are causing a catastrophic "greenhouse effect" that is overheating the earth. However, none of the alarmists bothers to mention that carbon dioxide amounts to only a tiny percentage of the atmosphere. Carbon dioxide is necessary for all plant life, and therefore all animal and human life to exist. There is a very small percentage of CO_2 in the atmosphere. CO_2 is only a trace gas. As of 2008, out of every hundred thousand molecules making up the atmosphere, only thirty-eight were CO_2 molecules.[22]

Remarkably, despite the growing alarms of AGW environmentalists who fear man-made global warming, it will take humanity's additional CO_2 emissions another five years to increase that number by 1 molecule out of 100,000 (to achieve 40 molecules, or 0.04 percent).

The atmosphere is primarily composed of nitrogen at 78.1 percent and oxygen at 20.9 percent. Together these gases form 99 percent of the atmosphere. Of the 1 percent of gases that form the rest of the earth's atmosphere, several trace gases are considered greenhouse gases because they act to moderate the climate. These greenhouse gases include (in order of concentration):

TRACE GASES IN OUR ATMOSPHERE
(Out of the 1% of Gases Left)

Greenhouse Gases	% of Greenhouse Gases
water vapor	95%+
carbon dioxide	0.038%
methane	0.0002%
nitrous oxide	0.00003%
ozone	0.000004%

To place this tiny percentage of CO_2 (0.038%) in some perspective; try this experiment:

Imagine that the earth's atmosphere is represented by an enormous roofed football stadium holding one million balloons, each white balloon represents a single one of one million gas molecules in our atmosphere. Virtually all of the balloons are white, representing primarily Nitrogen (at 78.1%=781,000) balloons and Oxygen (at 20.9%=209,000) balloons. The few balloons representing carbon dioxide molecules will be light green.

Of the total, how many of the one million balloons would be light green? Only 380 out of one million!

How many of the 380 light green balloons, representing carbon dioxide, would be manmade and thus dark green in color? Only three percent of the carbon dioxide in air is a result of human activity. The percentage of earth's atmosphere that is composed of carbon dioxide is only .0000114%. Therefore, only *twelve* out of one million balloons would signify the very miniscule portion of earth's atmosphere composed of CO_2 produced by humans![23]

The impact of all carbon dioxide on the greenhouse effect is itself minuscule, but humanity's contribution to CO_2 is much, much less. The overwhelming majority (97 percent) of carbon dioxide that is added annually to the atmosphere is produced by nature. Massive amounts of CO_2 are released annually by volcanoes, compost from vegetation, swamps, rice paddies, insects, and bacteria. In addition, massive amounts of CO_2 are constantly released or absorbed by the oceans annually, depending on the ocean's temperature. These natural processes have nothing to do with automobiles, coal-burning power plants, human use of air conditioning, or factories.

An article in the journal *Science* published November 5, 1982, documented that trillions of termites emit ten times more greenhouse gases than all human activities combined. Wetlands and swamps also release more greenhouse gases than all human activities. Remarkably, volcanoes emit hundreds of times more CO_2 than power plants. (There are approximately one hundred active volcanoes throughout the world.)

The largest single source of CO_2 emissions comes from the Pacific Ocean at the equator. Massive carbon dioxide sinks (or reservoirs) in the depths of the equatorial region of the oceans release approximately 70 percent of the earth's emissions of CO_2, while additional contributions arise from biological processes.[24] The human contribution of CO_2 is greatly overshadowed by these far larger, natural, and obviously uncontrollable sources of additional carbon dioxide to the atmosphere.

EVIDENCE FROM ACTUAL TEMPERATURE RECORDS

Consider the record of the rise in global air temperatures. During the sixty-year period between 1880 and 1940, the earth's temperature rose at a similar rate to the rise in atmospheric CO_2. However, during the following period—between 1940 and 1975—there was no increase in global temperature.[25] Note that the thirty-five-year period under consideration witnessed World War II and massive industrialization, including growth in nations that previously were not industrialized. While carbon dioxide levels rose significantly during that time, there was no corresponding increase in temperature.

Then, between 1975 and 1997, the gradual rise in temperature once again closely matched the rate of increase of atmospheric carbon dioxide.[26] However, from 1998 to the present, while the level of man-made CO_2 continued to rise every year, there was again no corresponding rise in temperature. In fact, the global temperature actually cooled by approximately 1°F during this most recent period.[27]

Many climate scientists believe we may be in for several decades of moderate cooling. The reality is that there is no consistent correlation between the levels of atmospheric CO_2 and global temperature.

The European Foundation report "Climate Change Is Natural: 100 Reasons" concluded that there was little, if any, warming based on greenhouse gases since 1979. "If one factors in non-greenhouse influences such as El Nino [sic] events and large volcanic eruptions, lower atmosphere satellite-based temperature measurements show little, if any, global warming since 1979, a period over which atmospheric CO_2 has increased by 55 ppm (17 percent)."[28]

THE POSITIVE EFFECTS OF INCREASED LEVELS OF CARBON DIOXIDE

The continually rising CO_2 levels are in fact our best hope of quickly raising crop yields to feed an ever-growing global population. The historical verified increase in the CO_2 content of our atmosphere (from 250 parts per million to today's 385 ppm) has significantly improved human nutrition by raising global crop yields. Increased amounts of atmospheric CO_2 in the future will greatly assist efforts to eliminate hunger in the Third World. This is one of the most suppressed stories of the positive impact of increased levels of CO_2.

Agricultural scientists know that the greater the percentage of CO_2 in the air, the less water is needed to grow crops. Wheat and corn have tiny pores known as stoma that absorb CO_2 from the air and let water vapor out. As levels of CO_2 in the air increase, the stomata shrink and additional water is retained by the plant crops. A doubling of CO_2 in the atmosphere will reduce the amount of water the plants require by approximately 50 percent.[29] Therefore, increasing levels of carbon dioxide in the atmosphere have a positive impact on agricultural production, especially in arid and semiarid regions. Drier agriculture regions will be able to grow significantly greater amounts of food to feed their growing populations.

WATER VAPOR: ANOTHER GLOBAL-WARMING CULPRIT

Carbon dioxide is a trace greenhouse gas, quite weak in its measurable impact on moderating atmospheric temperatures. It is far from being the major component that contributes to the greenhouse effect as AGW proponents suggest. Water vapor (not clouds) is a far more pervasive and active greenhouse gas, contributing at least 95 percent to any potential greenhouse effect.[30] The reason AGW alarmists don't discuss the far more significant water-vapor effect as the major contributor to the greenhouse effect is that there is nothing humanity can do to modify the level of water vapor in the atmosphere. The AGW movement chooses instead to focus on CO_2, since they can blame humanity for increasing its "carbon footprint." Opposition to carbon emissions can be used as leverage to regulate the activities of nations, corporations, and individuals. The myth that CO_2 is the most common and influential greenhouse gas has confused the debate because all greenhouse gases together form only 3 percent of the atmosphere by volume, and CO_2 itself constitutes only 0.038 percent of the atmosphere.

Meanwhile, 95 percent of the impact of greenhouse gases is contributed by natural water vapor and carbon dioxide produced by natural—not man-made—means. Human activities produce a minuscule percentage of the world's annual release of carbon dioxide. Some 95 percent of any greenhouse effect has nothing to do with human activities. Even if CO_2 did seriously impact global temperatures (it is still an unproven theory), engaging in enormously costly regulation and restriction of carbon dioxide emissions would have hardly any positive measurable effect, even according to the UN scientists' own calculations. That would be true even after ninety years of incredible economic pain, loss of our Western prosperity, significant reductions in the standard of living and quality of life, increased energy costs, and decreased industrial and agricultural production.

An apt slogan for the AGW movement's agenda is "All pain and no gain!"

International Climate Treaties and Fossil-Fuel Substitutes

T he United Nations has convened several international climate summits to reach agreement among nations on steps to take to combat the perceived global-warming problem. We have seen in previous climate treaties that self-appointed international bodies have used the global-warming issue as a pretext to violate the legal rights of sovereign nations. Nations that sign these climate treaties are ultimately sacrificing their national independence and subjecting themselves and their citizens to the dictates of an unelected international body. They are surrendering their sacred political duty to defend and protect the interests of their citizens without discussion or debate regarding this unprecedented surrender of democratic political rights.

The major climate summits of the past and the resulting international accords warrant a much closer examination. These include the 1997 Kyoto

Protocol and the 2009 Copenhagen Climate Change Accord. While on the surface the international climate-control agreements are designed to address the perceived problem of global warming, in truth they are legally binding international treaty negotiations whose chief goal is to legitimize and legalize a future global government. The president of the European Council, Herman Van Rompuy, described the Copenhagen climate summit as "another step towards the global management of our planet."[1]

The European Union (EU) enthusiastically endorsed its Kyoto Protocol obligations, but the EU has actually *increased* its carbon dioxide emissions by 13 percent, according to Lord Nigel Lawson of the British House of Lords (former Chancellor of the Exchequer under Margaret Thatcher). Remarkably, the EU can still claim environmental success by purchasing carbon offsets from China and other nations. The EU uses carbon offsets to pay other nations to destroy atmospheric pollutants such as CFC-23. (Some of the CFC-23 that was destroyed by China was cynically manufactured solely for the purpose of being destroyed, to attract carbon-offset money from the EU. This environmental policy is nothing but smoke and mirrors.)[2]

THE DESTRUCTIVE EFFECTS OF CLIMATE TREATIES

The 1997 Kyoto Protocol is designed to regulate and limit the man-made emissions of carbon dioxide, nitrous oxide, methane, sulfur hexafluoride, perfluorocarbons, and hydroflurocarbons. The 2009 Copenhagen Accord and the proposed terms of the 2010 United Nations Climate Change Conference in Cancún, Mexico, if fully implemented, would inevitably result in the following economic and social disasters:

- They will cause the destruction of tens of millions of U.S. jobs annually.

- They will cost the West hundreds of billions of dollars in lost economic production annually for the next *century*.
- They will seriously reduce or reverse economic growth in both the developed world and the Third World.
- They would seriously reduce the West's ability to raise the standard of living in the Third World from abject poverty into a lifestyle of relative prosperity and health.

The Kyoto Protocol

The language of the 1997 Kyoto Protocol requires that the "developed country Parties shall deeply cut their domestic GHG [greenhouse gases] emissions." *It declares that developed nations should transform their economies over the coming decades in order to collectively reduce by 2050 greenhouse gas emissions by 80 to 95 percent compared to 1990 levels.*

The United Nations Intergovernmental Panel on Climate Change (IPCC) Synthesis Report "Summary for Policymakers" contains the full Working Group III report. It lays out the 2020 and 2050 targets needed for Annex I (developed) countries, such as the United States and Canada. The following chart reveals the massive reductions of greenhouse emissions required by Kyoto from the original level in 1990 and the reduced emissions allowed in 2020 and in 2050 for Annex I (industrial) countries.

KYOTO PROTOCOL REQUIRED REDUCTIONS IN CO$_2$ EMISSIONS

Region	2020	2050
Annex I nations (industrialized nations)	−25% to −40%	−80% to −95%[3]

If the industrialized nations actually achieved this Kyoto Protocol goal, the standard of living experienced by the majority of people in the West would be reduced to approximately the level of the Great Depression. It is interesting to note that the Russian Academy of Sciences issued a report in May 2004 that came to the conclusion that *the scientific evidence and basis for the 1997 Kyoto Protocol is totally without scientific merit.*[4]

Most of the world's countries have signed and ratified the Kyoto Protocol. Though the United States signed the agreement in December 1998, it is the only industrialized nation not to have ratified the Protocol and therefore is not bound by it. President Bill Clinton and Vice President Al Gore never brought the document to Congress for ratification, and in 1997 the U.S. Senate passed the Byrd-Hagel resolution, which stated the Senate would never ratify the agreement if it caused economic hardships and if developing countries were not held to the same timetable.[5]

The Copenhagen Accord

The Copenhagen negotiations in December 2009 were a total disaster for the global-warming alarmist position. The Copenhagen meeting immediately followed the providentially but unauthorized release of thousands of e-mails and data files from the Climate Research Unit (CRU) of the University of East Anglia (UK) on November 20, 2009. The exposure of these documents on the Internet led to what has been called the Climategate scandal. The resulting chaotic meeting in Copenhagen concluded with a virtually meaningless, nonbinding, "let's meet again" memorandum that the participating countries "recognized" as having seen. No significant agreements on climate change were voted on or agreed to.

According to Greenpeace activist Joss Garman, the Copenhagen Accord is "beyond bad. It contains no legally binding targets and no indication of when or how they will come about. There is not even a declaration that the world will aim to keep global temperature rises below 2 C."[6]

Even the $100 billion global-climate fund that was agreed to at Copenhagen is virtually irrelevant. In fact, the fund is largely composed of existing, previously agreed-upon budget commitments of the various nations with very little new money committed.

THE UNITED STATES AND CLIMATE CHANGE

President Barack Obama pledged that the United States will by 2050 cut CO_2 emissions to the levels of 1910, when there were only 92 million Americans. By 2050, the Census Bureau estimates there will be almost 420 million Americans. Therefore, the president's commitment would mean that CO_2 emissions per capita in 2050 will have to be reduced to almost the level that existed in 1875! *This would basically destroy the American industrial economy, and devastate American employment and the nation's standard of living. And all of this sacrifice would be in vain, attempting to prevent a scientifically unverified environmental threat.* The true purpose, of course, is to achieve their hidden socialist-globalist goal of establishing a centralized socialist-Marxist world government.

The socialist leaders of many nations in the Third World and the globalist-oriented Western leaders of the United Nations have endorsed the policy of sending hundreds of billions of dollars annually to the Third World. This money is said to go primarily to national leaders to help them reduce the environmental impact of carbon dioxide emissions. However, investing only a fraction of that annual amount in clean water, sanitation, and medical care would produce an enormous improvement in the quality of life for the billions of people living in the Third World. Such an investment would dramatically improve the personal health, prosperity, and standards of living of billions of the poorest people on earth.

The IPCC has stated that proposed reductions in global carbon dioxide levels will prevent the rise of the average global temperature from exceeding 2°C (3.6°F) above levels experienced prior to the Industrial Revolution. *The planned carbon reductions would cost the world almost $40 trillion a year in reduced economic growth over each of the next ninety years.* But despite the staggering cost, the Kyoto Protocol will have only a very minimal impact on future temperature increases, even based on IPCC's projections. The anticipated reduction in global warming is based on a faulty projection.

UN climate scientists believe (without scientific evidence) that continuing growth in the levels of man-made CO_2 will raise the world's temperature in 2100 by as much as 10°F. They claim that to avoid such an increase, we need to enact economic self-destruction of our Western economy and your standard of living. Beyond that, we need to send $180 billion per year to Third World dictators to assist their carbon-reduction plans. What will be the global temperature improvement in exchange for the destruction of our Western economy and way of life? According to UN scientists who support the Kyoto Protocol, the major global-warming regulations, huge energy taxes, and major reductions in your family's standard of living will result in a miniscule reduction of just *one-third of 1°F* by the year 2100.

If a significant reduction in the earth's global temperature is obviously not the real goal, then what is the actual hidden agenda? The documented evidence presented in this book is overwhelming. The leaders of the AGW movement are using the global-warming deception to motivate politicians, media leaders, educators, and millions of citizens to surrender their freedoms and liberties in a vain plan to save the earth from an imagined human-caused global-warming threat.

Alternatives to the terms of the Kyoto Protocol
to Improve the Environment

In contrast to the UN's plans to combat AGW, there are several workable (and far less costly) alternatives that would truly benefit humanity. For example, we could spend $3 billion every year on mosquito nets, environmentally safe use of indoor DDT sprays, and subsidies for new medical therapies—and within ten years cut the number of malaria infections in the Third World by 50 percent. For the same amount of money it would take to save *just one life* utilizing carbon dioxide reductions, more intelligent, focused environmental policies could save 78,000 lives in ten years by combating malaria with DDT.

A group of environmental experts directed by the respected environmentalist Bjorn Lomborg, author of *The Skeptical Environmentalist* and *Cool It,* reviewed the 2009 Copenhagen Accord. They concluded that world leaders could help the planet far more effectively by focused investing in inexpensive targeted policies to combat malnutrition. One of the best social investments available includes the provision of micronutrients to provide significant improvements in the health of malnourished children in the Third World. The provision of micronutrients (especially vitamin A, iron, and zinc) given to the billion-plus undernourished children would require an investment of only $3 billion; a pittance compared to the estimated costs of the Kyoto Protocol ($100 billion annually). The economic gains from the expected improvements in productivity and general health would eventually save more than $1 billion every year.[7]

The investment of hundreds of millions of dollars in providing salt iodization would prevent the devastating disease of goiter. (Salt iodization is the substitution or addition of iodine atoms in organic compounds.) Investing millions every year in the iron fortification of diets in the Third World would eliminate the stunting of growth in many children as well as serious cognitive and other developmental problems.[8] Ten billion dollars invested every year on food aid and agricultural production would result in the feeding of more than two hundred million people who currently lack adequate nutrition. The investment of $4 billion annually would provide more than one billion people in the Third World access to clean drinking water and help 2.5 billion who live without adequate sanitation, preventing one billion people from contracting debilitating diarrhea every year.[9]

THE SOCIALIST NATURE OF CARBON TAXES

Those who support the AGW alarmist agenda argue that governments should immediately introduce a comprehensive cap-and-trade carbon tax and control system. In addition, the Kyoto Protocol calls for a massive redistribution of wealth from the taxpayers of the industrialized countries of the West to the leaders of the Third World. Carbon taxes would transfer billions of dollars from the West to Third World countries, where it will naturally end up in the hands of dictators and despots.

The practice of trading carbon credits has proved to be a colossal financial fraud and economic disaster in the European Union. The EU's Emission Trading System, which involves an elaborate cap-and-trade system, continues to disintegrate. James Kanter, writing for the *New York Times,* reports, "Carbon traders, for example, have been arrested for tax fraud; evidence has emerged of lucrative projects that may do nothing to curb climate change; and steel and cement companies have booked huge profits selling surplus permits they received for free."[10]

Carbon-credit trading is a complex financial-derivative scheme designed by some of the same fraud artists who brought about the billion-dollar collapse of the Enron Corporation. Carbon credits are completely unregulated, impossible to accurately track, and actually allow European businesses to duck out of complying with demands for carbon emissions reductions. They are allowed to "offset" their carbon emissions by paying for cuts to be made by other companies. In addition, cap-and-trade plans do not reduce in any way the emissions of man-made CO_2. The reality is that cap-and-trade policies have an entirely different purpose.

Hidden cap-and-trade policies

The first phase of the EU's Emission Trading System (EU ETS), from 2005 to 2007, was a failure. Fraudulent overallocation of permits to favored companies allowed those companies to pollute as well as to sell unused carbon credits to other firms. This led inevitably to a virtual price collapse from forty-one dollars to just twenty-five cents per ton of carbon dioxide, meaning the cap-and-trade system did not reduce carbon dioxide emissions at all.

U.S. senators John Kerry and Joe Lieberman introduced the misleadingly named American Power Act, while pretending that it was a climate bill or a job-creation bill. In reality, the bill was nothing less than a massive new tax bill on carbon dioxide emissions, creating direct and indirect taxes on coal, natural gas, oil, and gasoline. A report was issued on June 30, 2010, by the Institute for Energy Research in Washington, D.C. that documented the full economic impact of the Kerry-Lieberman American Power Act.

The American Power Act would **reduce U.S. employment by roughly 522,000** jobs in 2015, rising to over **5.1 million jobs by 2050**.

Households would face a gross annual burden of **$125.9 billion per year or $1,042 per household**, with costs disproportionately borne by low-income households.

On a net basis, the **top income quintile** [top 20 percent] **will benefit financially**, redistributing to these households roughly **$12.3 billion per year from the bottom 80 percent** of earners."[11]

A cap-and-trade policy would impose enormous annual energy and tax costs on all Americans via a carbon tax on all goods and services produced in the United States. The average family of four would pay $1,700 in additional taxes each year. It is also predicted that the United States would lose more than two million jobs directly as the result of cap-and-trade schemes.[12]

The 1,427-page cap-and-trade bill, known as the Waxman-Markey Climate Change Bill, was passed by the U.S. House of Representatives in 2009, with almost none of the Democrat or Republican members bothering to read the bill before voting. This bill is in truth America's "Economic Suicide Act." There are provisions in the bill that repeat some of the worst mistakes that occurred during the 2008 financial collapse. The bill includes 150 pages of provisions that would lower U.S. home values. Under this bill, when you sell your house, the windows, appliances, heating, air conditioning, and insulation would have to be inspected and approved for compliance with federal energy standards—at the homeowner's cost.

According to a report from the Center for Data Analysis at the Heritage Foundation, "Prices at the gas pump would leap 58%, and residential electricity costs would 'necessarily skyrocket' 90%. Total GDP loss by 2035 would be $9.4 trillion. Net job losses (after green job creation) could approach 2.5 million by 2035. Manufacturing loses about 1 million jobs in 2035."[13]

While cap-and-trade legislation ostensibly aims to reduce carbon dioxide emissions, the only thing that is actually capped is economic growth and the after-tax income of unfortunate citizens. The real cost of carbon credits is that businesses and consumers will end up paying a hidden carbon tax that is passed on to any user of energy. *Cap-and-tax policies* is a more accurate name because the policies would impact virtually every aspect of your life, including higher utility bills, higher taxes, higher gasoline prices, and major new restrictions in the form of new EPA regulations regarding the energy efficiency of your home and all factories. Cap-and-trade policies would reduce the energy supply at a time when America needs a safe and reliable domestic supply instead of undependable foreign sources.

A U.S. Treasury Department analysis concluded "that a cap and trade law would cost American taxpayers up to $200 billion a year, the equivalent of hiking personal income taxes by about 15 percent."[14] Welcome to the initial benefits of the man-made global-warming alarmist policy coming your way.

THE WAR ON FOSSIL FUELS

Amory Lovins of the Rocky Mountain Institute expressed the antitechnology, antienergy AGW philosophy that motivates many of those who embrace the global-warming alarmist cause. Lovins declared, "It'd be little short of disastrous for us to discover a source of clean, cheap, abundant energy, *because of what we could do with it.*"[15]

Paul Ehrlich, a professor at Stanford University, expressed his repudiation of any new developments that provide reliable and affordable energy to lift the poor inhabitants of the Third World out of poverty. Incredibly, Ehrlich warned that "giving society cheap, abundant energy would be the equivalent of giving an idiot child a machine gun."[16]

As one of the proposed solutions to global warming, Al Gore and others have promoted the development of wind farms and solar panels as alternatives to power provided by inexpensive and reliable fossil fuels. However, numerous studies reveal that wind farms and solar panels would do very little to reduce CO_2 emissions.

According to the U.S. Government Accountability Office, "Wind power accounted for only about one-tenth of 1 percent of total U.S. electric power generation capacity in 2003."[17] The U.S. government also reports that, at the present time, "solar power provides less than 1% of U.S. energy needs."[18]

Wind farms are not an efficient way to generate reliable electricity. Due to the variability of wind (and the subsequent 25 percent or less efficiency daily), the British Wind Energy Association accepts that a figure of 75 percent back-up coal-burning power is required to supplement wind power. As a result, the true cost of wind power is vastly greater than any other form of power. First you have the direct costs of generating wind-farm electrical power. Then you must build a fossil-fuel power plant to ensure continuous electrical energy when wind variations fail to energize the wind farm. The result is a very expensive and inefficient redundancy with much higher costs than using reliable and inexpensive hydroelectric, coal-burning, or nuclear-power generation plants.

Global Warming and Population Control

When you study the statements of the leading spokesmen for the anthropogenic global warming (AGW) movement, you quickly realize that their philosophy reaches far beyond a concern for protecting the human race from climate change. Ironically, in many instances the fight against global warming is closely aligned with a political effort to drastically *reduce* the earth's population. Remarkably, the quotations reveal a cold-blooded agenda to drastically reduce the earth's population, eliminating billions of people.

Statements made by certain AGW spokesmen suggest that they have a second agenda, with racist and religious overtones. This agenda is revealed in part through their stated desire to radically reduce the population of the earth. This radical goal applies especially to the population of the Third

World. Their population-reduction agenda is diabolical, immoral, and racist, and it must be exposed!

Dave Foreman, cofounder of the AGW-supporting Earth First!, declared, "My three main goals would be to reduce human population to about 100 million worldwide, destroy the industrial infrastructure and see wilderness, with its full complement of species, returning throughout the world."[1]

Admitting that you would like to eliminate more than 98 percent of the earth's population, while presenting yourself as working against global warming to "protect" the human race, is like Jack the Ripper offering his services as an emergency room surgeon. Inexpensive energy generated by fossil fuels is one of the key resources that is desperately needed by the billions living in the Third World to help lift people out of centuries of poverty, disease, and despair. But the champions of AGW are now working to prevent people throughout the Third World from receiving the benefits of cheap, reliable energy.

For those in the global-warming movement, it seems to be a short step from opposing carbon dioxide emissions to taking a stand against assisting the improvement of the life, economy, and health of Third World citizens. In a BBC interview, Sir James Lovelock commented on the earth's growing population. "The big threat to the planet is people: there are too many, doing too well economically and burning too much oil."[2] The antihumanity theme is developed further by Lovelock in his book *Healing Gaia: Practical Medicine for the Planet*. Lovelock wrote, "Humans on the Earth behave in some ways like a pathogenic micro-organism, or like the cells of a tumor."[3] In Lovelock's view, continued economic prosperity is a threat to the earth's survival. I am confident that the billions living in abject poverty would love to test his hypothesis and seek to live a full, prosperous life as best they can.

Billionaire Ted Turner, founder of CNN and a major United Nations donor (promising $1 billion in contributions), has repeatedly supported those who want to drastically reduce the earth's population. But how would such a population reduction be accomplished? No one explains the details of their diabolical plans. The twentieth century witnessed the tragic and evil deaths of more than 200 million people killed to achieve the political, economic, and racial goals of fascism and Communism. The history of genocide in the last century is chilling when we read about it. So what do the AGW movement supporters quoted in this chapter truly have in mind?

Prince Philip, Duke of Edinburgh and husband of Queen Elizabeth II, stated in a 1990 interview, "If I were reincarnated I would wish to be returned to earth as a killer virus to lower human population levels."[4]

The editor of *Earth First! Journal,* John Davis, made a remarkable and antihuman statement: "I suspect that eradicating small pox was wrong. It played an important part in balancing ecosystems."[5] Christopher Manes, also of Earth First!, declared his total contempt for humanity: "The extinction of the human species may not only be inevitable but a good thing."[6]

Other AGW supporters have espoused bans on childbirth and have endorsed the forced use of contraceptives. David Brower, founder of Friends of the Earth, is quoted in *The Coercive Utopians* making this statement: "Childbearing [should be] a punishable crime against society...all potential parents [should be] required to use contraceptive chemicals, the government issuing antidotes to citizens chosen for childbearing."[7]

THE ANTIHUMAN AND ANTI-GOD AGENDA

The evil antihuman philosophy of many of those who have allied themselves with global-warming alarmist groups reflects their deep and abiding hatred of humanity, as well as their utter disdain toward God as their Creator. A 1993 study, The First Global Revolution, done by the socialist-globalist Club of Rome concluded, "All these dangers [global warming] are caused by human intervention and it is only through changed attitudes and behavior that they can be overcome. *The real enemy, then, is humanity itself.*"[8]

Consider the full implications of that remarkable statement. If the world had not witnessed the Nazis' genocidal destruction of six million Jews during World War II and the Soviet genocide of thirty million Ukrainians, you might think the people and documents quoted are merely speaking theoretically. But history shows that genocide is carried out on a grand scale more often than we want to think.

In another Club of Rome document titled *Goals for Mankind,* we read, "The resultant ideal sustainable [human] population is hence more than 500 million but less than one billion."[9] Consider the true implications of this Club of Rome statement. *It suggests that more than five billion of earth's inhabitants should be killed!*

Michael Fox, vice president of the Humane Society, warned, "Mankind is the most dangerous, destructive, selfish and unethical animal on the earth."[10]

Paul W. Taylor, ethics professor at City University in New York City, revealed his cynical view regarding the value of human life. He wrote, "Given the total, absolute, and final disappearance of Homo Sapiens, then, not only would the Earth's Community of Life continue to exist but…the ending of the human epoch on Earth would most likely be greeted with a hearty 'Good riddance!'"[11]

Are the people who make such statements truly serious? I believe they are. And it's not just individuals and private organizations that are taking a stand against humanity. The United Nations, which receives billions of dollars in taxpayer money in the form of funding from the United States and Canada, has joined the population-limitation effort. The UN document titled *Global Biodiversity Assessment* included this sobering statement: "A reasonable estimate for an industrialized world society [population] at the present North American material standard of living would be 1 billion. At the more frugal European standard of living, 2 to 3 billion would be possible."[12]

PROPOSED SOLUTIONS TO THE "PROBLEM" OF OVERPOPULATION

If some AGW leaders support eliminating vast numbers of the human population, how do they propose doing so? How would they reduce the earth's population from 6.5 billion to 1 billion—or as little as 500 million? An astonishing editorial published in *The Economist* spoke of the total elimination of humanity as a potentially positive development. "The extinction of the human species may not only be inevitable, but a good thing."[13]

Paul Ehrlich, author of the book *The Population Bomb,* wrote, "A cancer is an uncontrolled multiplication of cells; the population explosion is an uncontrolled multiplication of people.... We must shift our efforts from treatment of the symptoms to the cutting out of the cancer.... We must have population control...by compulsion if voluntary methods fail."[14]

The famous oceanographer Jacques Cousteau suggested a more coercive, even violent, approach to population reduction. Cousteau was quoted by *The UNESCO Courier* speaking about the need to drastically reduce the earth's population. "One American tires the planet far more than twenty Bangladeshis.... It's terrible to have to say this. World population must be stabilized and to do that we must eliminate 350,000 people per day. This is so horrible to contemplate that we shouldn't even say it."[15]

A more circuitous strategy was suggested by Victor J. Yannacone Jr., an attorney and cofounder of the Environmental Defense Fund (EDF). Referring to EDF cofounder Dr. Charles Wurster at a May 20, 1970, speech at the Union League Club in New York City, Yannacone said, "A reporter asked Dr.

Wurster whether or not the ban on the use of DDT would not encourage the use of the very toxic alternative materials, Parathion, Azedrin and Methyl-parathion, the organophosphates, [and] nerve gas derivatives. And he said 'Probably.' The reporter then asked him if these organo-phosphates did not have a long record of killing people. And Dr. Wurster, reflecting the views of a number of other scientists, said 'So what? People are the cause of all the problems; we have too many of them; we need to get rid of some of them; and this is as good a way as any."[16]

Others seem to hold expectations for a deadly virus that might significantly reduce the human population worldwide. Open contempt for the lives of hundreds of millions of people living in the Third World is expressed frequently, including this cynical quote from the *Earth First! Journal:* "As radical environmentalists, we can see AIDS not as a problem but a necessary solution."[17]

National Park Service biologist David M. Graber, in a book review published in the *Los Angeles Times Book Review,* wrote, "We are not interested in the utility of a particular species, or free-flowing river, or ecosystem to mankind. They have...more value—to me—than another human body, or a billion of them.... Until such time as Homo Sapiens should decide to rejoin nature, some of us can only hope for the right virus to come along."[18]

None of the critics who feel the human population needs to be decimated has volunteered to commit suicide or to suggest friends or family members as volunteers to personally help reduce the human population. Many of the most extreme AGW alarmists hold tightly to an intellectual atheistic philosophy. This philosophy expresses its utter contempt for the lives, health, prosperity, hopes, and dreams of most other people on earth. They express contempt for the billions living in the Third World and demonstrate a profound selfishness that contradicts their professed love for the environment, which supports six and a half billion human beings.

Remarkably, many environmentalists seem quite willing to allow the undeveloped Third World to experience massive deaths due to starvation, rampant disease from waterborne germs, uncontrolled malaria, and tuberculosis that could be eradicated relatively easily through the use of available technology and the wise investment of only a few billion dollars in foreign aid.

THE WILDLANDS PROJECT: AN AGENDA TO RETURN NORTH AMERICA TO THE WILD

Expressing his deep animus toward capitalism and free-enterprise business expansion, David Foreman, the cofounder of Earth First!, wrote, "We must make this an insecure and inhospitable place for capitalists and their projects. We must reclaim the roads and plowed land, halt dam construction, tear down existing dams, free shackled rivers and return to wilderness millions of acres of presently settled land."[19]

The last two decades have seen massive numbers of new endangered-species listings, together with legal appeals and court cases intended to stop water development, mining, grazing, logging, and expanded recreational areas. Very often, these actions are well-coordinated efforts aimed at establishing a "regional reserve system which will ultimately tie the North American continent into a single Biodiversity Reserve."[20]

In his introduction to the Wildlands Project, Foreman, a radical environmentalist, explains that the project is designed to bring together grassroots conservation activists and environmentally focused nongovernmental organizations (NGOs). The stated vision is to protect and sustain native species and natural biosystems throughout North America. Foreman declares, "Our vision is continental...we seek to bring together conservationist [sic], ecologists, indigenous peoples, and others to protect and restore evolutionary processes and biodiversity." The Wildlands Project (now the Wildlands

Network) believes that existing natural areas such as national parks and government-owned tracts of wilderness are insufficient to protect the biodiversity of species because the existing areas are designed "to protect scenery and recreation, or to create outdoor zoos." Foreman then states that the "Wildlands Project in contrast calls for reserves established to protect wildlife habitat, biodiversity, ecological integrity, ecological service and evolutionary processes—that is vast interconnected areas of true wilderness." He added that they "see wilderness as the home for unfettered life, free from industrial human intervention." This wilderness will be "extensive areas of native vegetation in various successional stages, off-limits to human exploitation. Vast landscapes without roads, dams, motorized vehicles, powerlines, overflights, or other artifacts of civilization."[21]

More than one-half of the North American land mass is envisioned as making up this massive wilderness reserve system. Remarkably, most media have totally ignored this enormously costly and antihuman campaign.

The project calls for establishing vast core wilderness areas where human activity is totally prohibited. The wilderness areas would be linked together by biological corridors, so animals could travel from Alaska through western Canada to the western United States without ever seeing a human, a farm, a national park, or even a plane in the sky.

If you have ever wondered whether a radical environmentalist might be so loyal to the earth that he or she would embrace an outright antihuman philosophy, a rereading of the Foreman quotes should convince you.

The Wildlands Project's goals include seizing control of one-third to one-half of the United States and Canada. The group would block all access to humans and prohibit any human use of the protected areas. To get a clear picture of how much land area would be declared off-limits to the enjoyment of God's creation, see the map that shows the extent of the Wildlands Project's ambitions at www.discerningtoday.org/wildlands_map_of_us.htm.[22]

11

The Church of Global Warming

God appointed Adam and Eve, as the parents of humanity, to take care of the earth for the good of future humanity (see Genesis 1:28). Nowhere in Scripture does God allow humans to destroy His earth or to act with indifference toward the irreplaceable environment He created (see Genesis 1:31). Throughout the Old and New Testaments we find divine injunctions directing humanity to care for God's creation—to exercise dominion and to protect it. Christians should take seriously the responsibility to be good stewards of the earth and its environment.

Bible-believing Christians can be confident that humanity does not possess the power to destroy the earth—either gradually (through man-made climate change) or through sudden cataclysm (such as nuclear holocaust). God and only God holds the power to devastate the earth's environment. The earth's future is entirely in His hands.

While God commands His people to care for the earth, this is a far cry from considering the earth itself to be sacred, the source of life, or in any way deserving of our worship. Extreme environmentalist views have influenced people who are concerned about global warming to adopt a form of pagan idolatry. In many ancient cultures, animism flourished. The people chose to worship the "gods" of the sun, moon, trees, and the earth itself. However, the Scriptures make it clear that God Himself, who created the universe, is to be worshiped, not His creation. This truth is ignored by many in the anthropogenic global warming (AGW) movement.

For many, the AGW cause has taken on elements of a pagan religion. The God-given rights of humanity are considered by some environmental extremists as secondary to the assumed "rights" of millions of nonhuman species. In this odd inversion of values, God and His supreme creation—humanity—take a backseat to the imaginary spirit of the planet Earth, Gaia. The millions of plant and animal species are regarded as possessing greater value and significance than humanity.

IS GLOBAL WARMING A NEW RELIGION?

The apostle Paul described the spiritual apostasy that would arise in the "last days" generation, which would witness the return of Jesus Christ. Paul warned that many would deny the fact of God's creation of the universe, the earth, and the staggering number of species. In fact, he warned that for the first time, many would deny that there was a divine Creator. Instead, they would bow down to worship the creation. The earth and its manifold species would receive the honor and worship that God alone deserves. Paul wrote,

> For the invisible things of him [God] from the creation of the world
> are clearly seen, being understood by the things that are made, even

his eternal power and Godhead; so that they [humanity] are without excuse:... Wherefore God also gave them up to uncleanness through the lusts of their own hearts, to dishonor their own bodies between themselves: Who changed the truth of God into a lie, and worshipped and served the creature more than the Creator, who is blessed for ever. Amen. (Romans 1:20, 24–25)

One of the motivations for those who reject faith in God as the Creator is their hope that they will be able to escape God's judgment at the end of their earthly life. They have rejected the Bible's teaching that all of us, after death, will be forced to stand before God and account for our actions and motives. "And as it is appointed unto men once to die, but after this the judgment" (Hebrews 9:27).

It is evident to those who place their faith in Jesus Christ and who know the Scriptures that radical environmentalism has corrupted what began as a legitimate concern for the environment. For many, a commitment to combat global warming has turned into a pagan religion that opposes Judeo-Christian beliefs and denies God. Michael Barone wrote a fascinating article for the *Washington Examiner* titled "How Climate-Change Fanatics Corrupted Science." Here is his description of the corruption brought about by environmental fanaticism:

> The secular religion of global warming has all the elements of a religious faith: original sin (we are polluting the planet), ritual (separate your waste for recycling), redemption (renounce economic growth) and the sale of indulgences (carbon offsets). We are told that we must have faith (all argument must end, as Al Gore likes to say) and must persecute heretics (global warming skeptics are like Holocaust deniers, we are told).[1]

An essential component of most religions is the concept of sin, a basic transgression in thought or deed that renders us guilty and in need of forgiveness. The global-warming religion teaches that the original sin of humanity is our misuse of carbon dioxide. However, the chemical basis of all life on earth is carbon. Without carbon dioxide, no plant life and consequently no animal or human life could exist. Every nutrient that we consume ultimately depends on the existence of ample amounts of atmospheric carbon dioxide. Perversely, the CO_2 in our atmosphere that makes our life possible has recently been declared to be "pollution" by the U.S. Environmental Protection Agency (EPA).[2] The news media regularly runs stories about "carbon dioxide pollution," in which CO_2 is vilified as the "toxic enemy of humanity."

Historically, religion's antidote to sin is forgiveness. During the terrible corruption of biblical truth of Christianity during the Middle Ages, the truths of the Bible were lost to most Christians. At that time, the written Scriptures were available only in Latin, and most people (even priests) could not read the Bible. Tragically, most were ignorant of the doctrine of free salvation based solely on faith in Jesus Christ's forgiveness of our sins as taught in the Scriptures. Greed and guilt allowed the medieval church to sell indulgences to wealthy individuals who wanted to buy their way out of guilt and avoid being judged for their sins after death. Wealthy sinners believed that indulgences, pieces of paper purchased at great cost from church leaders, would free them from future condemnation and God's judgment.

The religious parallel to papal indulgences are the carbon offsets that corporations and individuals can purchase from foundations and carbon exchanges owned and organized by people such as Al Gore. A carbon offset is a financial instrument that ostensibly aids in the reduction of greenhouse gas emissions, especially CO_2. Carbon offsets are measured in metric tons of carbon dioxide or its equivalent mass in another greenhouse gas, such as methane. One carbon offset represents the reduction of one metric ton of carbon dioxide or its equivalent. Individuals or companies purchase carbon offsets to mitigate or offset their own greenhouse gas emissions. They seek to offset their use of transportation, electricity, and other activities that rely on the use of fossil fuels. In 2008, $705 million in carbon offsets were purchased in Europe and North America, representing some 123 million metric tons of CO_2 reductions.[3]

Usually, carbon offsets are sold by a company or foundation that promises to invest the funds in short- or long-term projects designed to reduce the emission of greenhouse gases through the use of alternative renewable energy. When a person or company purchases a carbon offset, they are paying to reduce greenhouse emissions by other individuals or companies rather than changing their own habits. The two major North American carbon-offset providers are the Bonneville Environmental Foundation (BEF) and the Climate Trust.

In order to qualify as a genuine carbon offset, two criteria must be met. The first is called *additionality:* the project would not have been completed unless carbon-offset funds were invested in the project. The second principle involves the proper *monitoring and verification* of the measurable environmental results. If these two criteria are not met, then the carbon offset is not a real reduction in greenhouse gas emissions; it is purely a scam.

Todd Wynn of the Cascade Policy Institute wrote about the fraudulent claims of those who promote carbon-offset projects without meeting the two essential criteria.

Now, investigations into two of the most prominent carbon offset providers in the U.S. have revealed that neither of them actually offers real reductions in greenhouse gas (GHG) emissions....

BEF [Bonneville Environmental Foundation] carbon offset funds paid for projects that were already going to be built, did not reduce emissions directly or at all, and used a portion of the proceeds for watershed restoration (not for offsetting emissions).[4]

THE GROWTH OF A GLOBAL-WARMING ENVIRONMENTAL RELIGION

All new religions seek to grow by means of conversion. The enthusiastic evangelism of those who embrace AGW adds new believers as it reinforces the faith of those who already believe. Certainly Al Gore would qualify as the main environmental missionary.

Gore and many of the leading enthusiasts who preach that the rest of us need to repent of our environmental sins behave in reality as classic hypocrites. For example, Gore's personal lifestyle is responsible for producing more than twenty times the carbon dioxide of the average American family.[5] But, of course, he has paid for his carbon "sins" through indulgence-like carbon offsets—purchased from his own company!

Another practice of the earth-worshiping religion is its mistreatment of those who refuse to embrace its dogmas. Many in the global-warming alarmist camp condemn as infidels those who fail to accept the new religion. Further, any who subsequently lose their enthusiasm for outlawing man-made global warming—or dare to reject some of the movement's extremist solutions—are vilified as apostates. Environmentalist Bjorn Lomborg, who wrote *The Skeptical Environmentalist,* was bold enough to suggest that other global problems—such as AIDS, malaria, and the lack of access to clean water—were global problems deserving of a priority response ahead of AGW.[6] Lomborg has been vilified as a heretic by his former environmental-extremist friends.

History reveals that poorer societies are more likely to suffer from degraded environmental conditions. It is generally only when a society reaches a level of widespread prosperity that serious investments are made in cleaning up the environment. Lomborg points out in his book *Cool It* that United Nations economists believe that citizens in both the developed and developing world will experience massive increases in income level by 2100. For example, income levels in the developing world are expected to rise twelve times higher than their 2010 levels. Lomborg projects that the average person living in the developed world ninety years from now will earn approximately $100,000 annually (in 2010 dollars). Just as wealthy Europeans and North Americans following the recovery from World War II became concerned about improving the environment, Lomborg concludes that as the developing nations increase their incomes, they will join the West in investing in improving the environment. Lomborg suggests we focus on solving more immediate challenges, including malaria, tuberculosis, AIDS, and lack of sanitation and clean drinking water, as well as supplying micronutrients that prevent many debilitating diseases. He says that if scientific evidence reveals serious growth in global temperature over the next several decades, our greatly increased wealth and tax revenues will make it easier to deal with the challenge of serious climate change.[7]

Patrick Moore, one of the founders of Greenpeace, abandoned his enthusiasm for global-warming alarmism as he became increasingly concerned about the movement's deeply held antipopulation propaganda and its extreme antiscientific attitudes.[8] Remarkably, Moore's old friends in Greenpeace and the larger AGW community then treated him as a traitor.

Traits of a cult

The global-warming religion has become a cult that demands absolute adherence to a radical environmental dogma. Followers must worship the earth and even an imaginary earth spirit known as Gaia, as suggested by Sir James Lovelock in his writing, *Healing Gaia*. Adherents believe Gaia embodies the spiritual force animating the planet.

The late Michael Crichton, an insightful writer about trends in science, was the first major writer to identify environmentalism and the AGW campaign as a new pagan religion. In a speech he delivered in 2003 and in his brilliant 2004 novel *State of Fear*, he shared his observations. In his speech, Crichton stated, "One of the most powerful religions in the Western World is environmentalism. Environmentalism seems to be the religion of choice for urban atheists…. Why do I say it's a religion? Well, just look at the beliefs. If you look carefully, you see that environmentalism is in fact a perfect 21st century remapping of traditional Judeo-Christian beliefs and myths."[9]

Crichton's novel *State of Fear* was one of the first popular books to explore the claimed scientific evidence and the propaganda arguments that extreme environmentalists embrace. The hidden political agenda behind AGW would eventually push the world's governments (especially the United States, Canada, and the European Union) to embrace the most extreme socially, politically, and economically destructive environmental policies. Crichton realized that the man-made global-warming agenda is supported by remarkably biased studies produced by scientists who often express a socialist-Marxist and globalist agenda. The scientists, far from using the objective scientific method to uncover new climate knowledge, were working instead to politically and economically transform America, Canada, and the European Union into a socialistic-globalist economy and society.

This global-warming religion's philosophical goal is to replace the Judeo-Christian religion, which made possible the great philosophical, religious, economic, and political foundations of Western civilization. A great number of people, especially college-educated leaders in politics, education, and business, have rejected the Judeo-Christian faith and worldview. In search of a new spiritual identity, many have embraced the paganism of Gaia, the spirit of the earth. In line with that, they have adopted values that seek above all to reverse man-made global warming and to reject Judeo-Christian values. Just as nature hates a vacuum, when people reject the Christianity of their parents' generation, they are compelled to find an alternative religious worldview.

A RELIGION THAT REJECTS VERIFIABLE TRUTH

The global-warming belief system displays the fundamental characteristics of an anti-Christian religion. It is not a serious scientific theory nor is it supported by significant verifiable scientific evidence. Judeo-Christian beliefs are unique among the religions of the world in that they are based on historically verifiable events. Meanwhile, the essential feature of most other religions is the claim by their leaders that the declarations and pronouncements of the religion must be accepted on the basis of "blind faith." If someone seriously questions those declarations, they place themselves outside the faith and in opposition to the group, which makes that person an enemy on some level. In all religions, those who doubt and repeatedly raise questions regarding fundamental beliefs and teachings are rejected by the leadership and are subsequently ostracized. Relentless attacks on the Judeo-Christian philosophy form a significant part of the propaganda message of this new AGW religion.

Global-warming "Nuremberg trials"

Some who embrace the AGW religion go on the attack when they encounter anyone who fails to accept the pagan global-warming religion. This is the way most religions have responded to those who dispute any of their significant doctrines. We often see personal attacks against anyone in the mass media or the scientific community who questions the so-called scientific consensus supporting the theory of man-made global warming.

As an example, Dr. Heidi Cullen, the most prominent climatologist for the Weather Channel, suggested that the American Meteorological Society should rescind its endorsement of the academic credentials of any television weather announcer who expressed skepticism regarding AGW.[10] This would be a career killer for any weather announcer. Internet blogger Dave Roberts, who writes for the Grist Web site, demanded the equivalent of war-crimes trials for any who reject the man-made global-warming claims: "When we've finally gotten serious about global warming, when the impacts are really hitting us and we're in a full worldwide scramble to minimize the damage, we should have war-crimes trials for these [expletive deleted]—some sort of climate Nuremberg."[11]

On CBS's *60 Minutes,* commentator Scott Pelley suggested that global-warming skeptics were equivalent to people who deny that the Nazis killed six million Jews during World War II.[12]

Using the same pejorative allusion, former Vice President Al Gore called skeptics "global-warming deniers." Gore stated, "Fifteen percent of the population believe the moon landing was actually staged in a movie lot in Arizona and somewhat fewer still believe the earth is flat. I think they all get together with the global warming deniers on a Saturday night and party."[13]

As a result of these attacks, many climatologists and well-respected meteorologists have been intimidated into silence. They fear they will lose friends, their careers, government and foundation grants, and in many cases academic tenure. Those who harbor skepticism toward man-made global warming have learned to be very careful about expressing their doubts publicly.

The global-warming religion has subverted even an institution as respected as England's Royal Society, founded more than three centuries ago as a significant part of England's growing scientific tradition. Its motto, "On the Word of No One," was a bold statement that the institution demanded that conclusions be based on scientific research and facts, not on personal preference, opinion, or someone's authority. Now the left-wing environmentalist movement has effectively captured the leadership and most of the senior membership of the Royal Society. They have, in effect, dismissed the need for research and debate by declaring, "The science is settled. The debate is over."

Indications of the fundamental religious nature of the global-warming issue are revealed by numerous statements. Richard Cizik, a former executive for the National Association of Evangelicals, stated, "Climate change isn't just a scientific question. It's a moral, a religious, a cosmological question. It involves everything we are and what we have a right to do."[14]

Richard Lindzen is a professor at the Massachusetts Institute of Technology's Department of Earth, Atmospheric, and Planetary Sciences. Lindzen gave a speech titled "Climate Alarmism: The Misuse of 'Science'" to the National Press Club in Washington, D.C. He spoke about public opinion surveys that ask questions such as these, "Do you believe in global warming? That is a religious question. So is the second part: Are you a skeptic or a believer?"[15]

Lord Nigel Lawson was formerly the Lord Chancellor to UK prime minister Margaret Thatcher. In a lecture he declared, "The new priests are scientists (well rewarded with research grants for their pains) rather than clerics of the established religions, and the new religion is eco-fundamentalism. But it is a distinction without much of a difference. And the old religions have not been slow to make common cause."[16]

ENVIRONMENTAL RELIGION AND GLOBAL GOVERNMENT

An analysis of the environmental religion that embraces the most extreme view of eco-fundamentalism reveals three serious threats to Judeo-Christian philosophical values and the capitalist attitudes that created the standard of living of Western culture.

The first threat is to the governments and economies of the European Union (EU) and North America. A wholesale adoption of the economic and environmental policies endorsed by the United Nations Intergovernmental Panel on Climate Change (IPCC), including its cap-and-trade policies, will lead to enormous economic and social losses that will inevitably produce another Great Depression.

The second threat is that the environmental religion is enormously hostile to capitalism and a free-market economy. The history of the last three centuries reveals that the only proven, sustainable, and reliable economic system for lifting the masses out of poverty is the free-enterprise system. Entrepreneurs and investors must have the freedom to make decisions and the latitude to do business without undue government interference.

The current growth of prosperous societies in Europe, Russia, China, Asia, and North and South America is the result of the development of free-market businesses. Hundreds of millions of people living in the undeveloped world are finally achieving previously unimaginable levels of health, clean water, wealth, education, and a significantly improved quality of life. When individuals are free to create businesses, they create wealth for themselves and their employees and generate taxes to support a social safety net.

The third threat is even greater: the progressive abandonment, especially among young adults, of the Judeo-Christian principles that built Western civilization. Millions have succumbed to AGW propaganda and have abandoned the tests of reason. Instead, they have embraced blind faith in the man-made global-warming religion. People are abandoning logic and reason regarding the environment and are rejecting the Judeo-Christian tradition at the same time the West is under violent attack by extremist elements in radical Islam.

J. R. Dunn wrote about the true nature of the global-warming movement as a pseudo-religion. As such, he argues, the movement promotes an imminent apocalypse, a fast-approaching end of the world as we know it. He wrote, "Another item that a pseudo-religion *must* have is an apocalypse—and that's what global warming is all about. In fact, the apocalyptic is the major fulcrum of environmentalism, the axis around which everything else turns."[17]

To preserve the fundamental biblical values that produced our liberty, economic freedom, and national independence, we must examine the implications behind the global-warming deception. It is urgent that we engage in a fundamental national debate about the scientific evidence for and against man-made global warming. In addition, we must examine the hidden socialist and global government agenda of the leaders of this movement that seeks to radically transform both our economy and our society.

GLOBAL WARMING AND BIBLICAL PROPHECY

What is the true goal of the pagan religion of eco-fundamentalism? The movement is not content to destroy our economic and political freedoms. Our fundamental Judeo-Christian beliefs and ideals also are being targeted.

The book of Revelation warns of a pagan religion that will emerge in the last-days generation. The false religion is referred to as Mystery Babylon. "Come, I will show you the judgment of the great harlot who sits on many waters, with whom the kings of the earth committed fornication, and the inhabitants of the earth were made drunk with the wine of her fornication" (Revelation 17:1–2, NKJV).

Today we can see the beginnings of the pagan, global, ecumenical church that will ultimately fulfill this prophecy. The coming Antichrist will make use of this worldwide ecumenical church to consolidate his global government. He will use the false church to entice and ensnare humanity into supporting his global government. The prophet John saw a vision of the apostate church of the last days grown rich and powerful in alliance with the global dictator, the Antichrist.

The false church will persecute and kill the Tribulation-period believers in Christ who will reject the apostate doctrines. John described the Scarlet Woman: "On her forehead a name was written: MYSTERY, BABYLON THE GREAT, THE MOTHER OF HARLOTS AND OF THE ABOMINATIONS OF THE EARTH" (Revelation 17:5, NKJV). The Roman writer Seneca wrote in his *Controversies* (5.1) that the harlots of Rome wore a nameplate or label on their foreheads. The book of Revelation describes a future unholy alliance between the rising political power of the Antichrist's ten-nation confederacy and the global ecumenical church of the last days. The Scarlet Woman, the Great Whore of Babylon, is a prophetic symbol of religious apostasy that represents the apostate church of the end times. This false church will prostitute itself to help the Antichrist consolidate his evil totalitarian power.

The role of the ecumenical church will involve the spiritual and intellectual preparation of the world's population to accept the rule of a new global Caesar. However, the Bible declares that, after achieving and consolidating his world power, the Antichrist and his ten allied nations will destroy the false church. This has historically been the modus operandi of dictators and megalomaniacs. Your close allies must be killed once you obtain supreme power because they are now the only potential challengers to your power.

In Revelation 17:16 we read, "And the ten horns which you saw on the beast, these will hate the harlot, make her desolate and naked, eat her flesh and burn her with fire" (NKJV). Note that the global dictator and the ten kingdoms of the revived Roman Empire turn on the false church and utterly destroy her with fire. We need to remember, however, that the Bible promises Christians that the supernatural resurrection of all living followers of Christ will occur before the beginning of the terrible seven-year Tribulation, which will begin with the global dictator, the Antichrist, signing a seven-year treaty with Israel (see Daniel 9:24–27).

When Satan totally possesses the soul of the Antichrist at the midpoint of the seven-year Tribulation period, he will defile the rebuilt Temple and then, for the first time, demand that all men and women worship him as "god" (see Revelation 13:5–8). After he benefits from the false church's propaganda support to consolidate his global government, the Antichrist and his allies will turn against the false church (see Revelation 17:16). At that point, everyone on earth will be compelled to worship the Antichrist as "god" or they will face death by beheading (see Revelation 20:4).

Origin of the Mystery Babylon religion

The key to the Babylonian worship system is the exaltation of the individual "to become like god" by means of a mysterious initiation, secret rituals, and mystic knowledge. This same demonic system motivated every ancient and modern false religion as well as numerous New Age cults.

This mysterious, pagan, earth-worshiping cult was a continual temptation and snare for the children of Israel. Despite their miraculous exodus from slavery in Egypt, they became afraid in the vast wilderness of Sinai and created a golden calf as an idol (see Exodus 32). The pagan worship of Babylon was always surrounded by idolatry, spiritualism, fornication, and the killing of righteous believers who rejected the satanic religion. The emerging global-warming religion involving the worship of Gaia, the earth-mother goddess, is the fulfillment of the Bible's prophecy of the resurgence of the Mystery Babylon religion.

The Gentile nations that surrounded Israel were continually seduced to go to "the high places" to engage in fornication with pagan priestesses and to practice idol worship of Baal. This was true from the time of the judges (see

Judges 2:11–13) until the days of the prophet Jeremiah (see 2 Chronicles 36:
20–21) leading up to the Babylonian captivity of the people of Israel.

> And them that had escaped from the sword carried he [Nebuchadnez-
> zar] away to Babylon; where they were servants to him and his sons
> until the reign of the kingdom of Persia: To fulfill the word of the
> Lord by the mouth of Jeremiah, until the land had enjoyed her
> sabbaths: for as long as she lay desolate she kept sabbath, to fulfil
> threescore and ten years.

The coming ecumenical religion

Following the future resurrection (Rapture) of all living Christians to heaven,
the many religions and false cults throughout the world will unite and create
the greatest worldwide, ecumenical religious system in history. This will en-
compass church denominations and world religions, including unbelieving
Protestants, Roman Catholics, and Greek and Russian Orthodox in addition
to Muslims, Hindus, Buddhists, and the growing New Age cults. All will
enthusiastically join forces with the rising Antichrist to bring about the greatest consolidation of political and religious power ever seen. With no living
born-again Christian believers left on earth to oppose it, this religious mon-
strosity will become the global superchurch that the book of Revelation calls
Mystery Babylon.

In Malachi Martin's insightful book *The Keys of This Blood,* he provides
evidence that Pope John Paul II began an unprecedented ecumenical campaign to unify all religions and spiritual movements under the leadership of
the Catholic Church. Today, the Vatican is continuing its campaign to establish the primacy of their Catholic Church over the emerging worldwide ecumenical church.[18] The goal is to obtain the organizational leadership authority over the spiritual and religious aspects of the coming global government.

The papacy publicly rejects both Marxism and free-market capitalism as unacceptable economic models for the emerging world order. The Vatican desires to create a new spiritual-political model for Europe and Russia based on a new "green" environmental-Catholic-socialist religious philosophy.[19] They hope to join this area with Catholic-dominated South America and Central America, and the "Christian–New Age ecumenically oriented" religious groups in North America.

A profound, behind-the-scenes decision by the papacy was first made during the final Vatican II session in 1965. It was decided that future ecumenical activities would reach out to and include all other Christian denominations and, for the first time, Muslims and Jews. Later, in a logical extension of this ecumenical revolution, attempts were made to approach Buddhists, American Indians, Shintoists, and New Age believers to invite them into the fold. The only groups that have successfully resisted the ecumenical entreaties are fundamentalist, Bible-believing Christians, and evangelical and charismatic/Pentecostal Christians.

In 1965 Pope Paul VI told the Vatican II Council that the Catholic Church would henceforth focus on the hopes, fears, and aspirations of humanity in this life, rather than the biblical focus on our spiritual condition in light of our heavenly destiny. As Malachi Martin wrote in *The Keys of This Blood,* Pope Paul VI concluded Vatican II with this focus: "to opt for man, to serve man, to help him build his home on this earth. Man with his ideas and his aims, man with his hopes and his fears, man in his difficulties and sufferings that was the centerpiece of the Church's interest."[20] Other popes, including the current Pope Benedict XVI, continued this ecumenical revolution while creating a profound shift in global religious systems. During the last ten years, high representatives of the Vatican have met with numerous religious leaders from virtually every Christian denomination as well as Muslims, Jews, Hindus, Buddhists, Sikhs, and Shintoists.

Over the last decade there have been many ecumenical discussions between the Roman Catholic Church, the Greek and Russian Orthodox Churches, and the Church of England. It has been taken for granted that the ultimate global spiritual leadership will be exercised by Rome. The Bible describes the false worldwide church of the last days in association with the ancient city of Rome. In Revelation 17:9 John declares, "Here is the mind which hath wisdom. The seven heads are seven mountains, on which the woman sitteth." The city of Rome was known from ancient times for its seven hills. To eliminate all possible doubt, John concludes his prophetic vision with these words: "And the woman which thou sawest is that great city, which reigneth over the kings of the earth" (Revelation 17:18).

The Bible's prophecies in Daniel 2 and Revelation 13 make it abundantly clear that the capital of the revived Roman Empire of the future global dictator, the Antichrist, will be the city of Rome. In their New Testament writings, the apostles called ancient Rome *Babylon* (see 1 Peter 5:13). The "great whore" (Revelation 17:1; 19:2) of the future will be Rome. This prophetic interpretation does not suggest, however, that the papacy and the Roman Catholic Church will be the only participants in the coming false church of the seven-year Tribulation. Every religious group in the world will join together once the true Christian believers in every denomination have been resurrected to heaven.

Hundreds of ecumenical groups in every nation have already joined in the effort to create a one-world church. It is a humanist, environmentally oriented, ecumenical group that is opposed to the Judeo-Christian values as taught in the Bible. Ironically, a group of religious leaders met in 1988 to plan the one-world church on the isle of Patmos, where John received his remarkable prophetic vision of the Great Whore of Babylon nineteen centuries ago.

Leaders of the Roman Catholic Church along with the Greek Orthodox Patriarch of Constantinople, together with Buddhists, met at the World

Conference of Religions for Peace to coordinate plans for the worldwide ecumenical movement. As an example of how far the process has progressed, consider the following: Catholic cardinals joined mainline Protestants and Jewish clergy in New York's famous St. Patrick's Cathedral (Roman Catholic) to honor the Dalai Lama, the global leader of Tibetan Buddhists.

The ultimate goal of these ecumenical movements is to unite people without regard to any particular religious belief system. The fascinating truth about the ecumenical religious leaders is that they are tolerant about *virtually* all beliefs. The only people they oppose are born-again Christians who believe there are fundamental biblical truths that must not be compromised. There is an interesting parallel with ancient Rome, which accepted all religions equally, no matter how bizarre. The only group pagan Rome attacked was the Christians, because they believed that Jesus was God and the Bible was the divinely inspired authority on spiritual matters. The pagans then, and now, hate Christians for their supposed "intolerance" of other religions' falsehoods.

Today, television talk shows will discuss the most absurd religious views with respect and tolerance. However, if a Christian says that Jesus is the Son of God and the Bible is true, the audience will criticize the Christian as an "intolerant bigot." Millions are taught that all religious beliefs are equally true and that as long as you are sincere, "God will accept you." Just as Rome hated the Christians, the rising false church will persecute the Jewish and Gentile Tribulation believers who will proclaim the "testimony of Jesus" during the seven-year Tribulation period.

The emergence of the Mystery Babylon religion

There is a growing consensus among religious leaders around the world that the various nations and religions need to unite to solve the great problems facing humanity. This Mystery Babylon religious system will be based on the

Babylonian satanic principle that "we can become like god" and control the earth's environment. This is the great self-realization movement we see manifested in the New Age influence throughout religious and cultural movements today.

Many of those supporting the global-warming movement are seeking alliances among the world's religions. The pantheistic religions of the American Indians, Buddhists, and animist belief systems are very attractive to New Age leaders. As an example, former Vice President Al Gore in his 1992 book *Earth in the Balance* makes it clear that he admires the pantheistic vision that identifies the earth as our Mother Goddess. He quotes with approval James Lovelock's Gaia hypothesis that suggests that the earth and its interlocking ecosystems are actually a living creature with intelligence and purpose.[21] This is pantheism taken to an extreme. Gore also suggests that we must harness the religious motivations of all humanity into "a single central organizing principle of civilization" to save the earth from environmental disaster.[22] While many Christians, such as myself, have been lifelong conservationists, we do not believe the heresy that the earth and its life forms are actually divine religious beings that we should worship and serve. We appreciate God's wonderful creation, but we worship only our divine Creator-God.

The extreme environmental pagan religion is a return to the kind of idolatry that the Old Testament prophets denounced. In his discussion of his belief that God exists in the earth and in all life, Al Gore asked the rhetorical question: "Why does it feel faintly heretical to a Christian to suppose that God is in us as human beings?"[23] The clear answer is that this New Age environmental religious belief *is* heresy. It is a direct violation of the Word of God. The Scripture declares, "I am God, and there is none like me" (Isaiah 46:9).

The heresy of pantheism, which holds that the earth is actually part of God, stands in total opposition to the teaching of the Bible. The apostle Paul declares that Jesus Christ is the Creator of the universe—He is not part of the universe. He created it out of nothing. "For by him [Jesus] were all things created, that are in heaven, and that are in earth, visible and invisible, whether they be thrones, or dominions, or principalities, or powers: all things were created by him, and for him: and he is before all things, and by him all things consist" (Colossians 1:16–17). Yet, just as the prophets declared, in these last days, earth worship, idolatry, pantheism, and paganism are on the rise everywhere.

Paul warned us that people would arise in the last days "who changed the truth of God into a lie, and worshipped and served the creature more than the Creator, who is blessed for ever. Amen" (Romans 1:25). This is happening all around us. We are living in the last days.

12

The Ongoing Global-Warming Challenge

After more than two decades of political maneuvering, media-backed propaganda efforts, and climate-change education programs, the man-made global-warming alarmist position is widely accepted by the general public. Most people simply assume that humanity's use of fossil fuels is gradually causing the planet to overheat. However, as more evidence comes to light, it is abundantly clear that the UN-affiliated scientific community has established this so-called scientific "fact" based on exaggeration, deception, and manipulation of data.

If an environmental catastrophe is imminent, it won't be caused by power plants and factories that run on fossil fuels. And it won't happen because you drive your car to work—even if you don't carpool. Changes in the earth's temperature are not unprecedented, and far more dramatic temperature shifts were taking place in past ages when humanity was doing nothing to add carbon dioxide to the atmosphere. The good news for people who support honest scientific inquiry is that more climate scientists are now willing to consider evidence that argues against the conclusions of the United Nations Intergovernmental Panel on Climate Change (IPCC). The research that the anthropogenic global warming (AGW) movement tries to discount and even silence shows that the earth's climate is impacted primarily by natural processes. Global temperature changes are triggered by solar radiation, the influence of cloud cover, and the moderating effects from all the greenhouse gases, including water vapor. Carbon dioxide is one very small factor in the process.

Lord Robert May, past president of the United Kingdom's prestigious Royal Society, once declared, "The debate on climate change is over." This unscientific claim was a mirror image of Al Gore's repeated declaration, "The science is settled." However, genuine science is always introducing and testing new theories and reevaluating past theories in light of new discoveries. Fortunately the Royal Society recently admitted, "Any public perception that science is somehow fully settled is wholly incorrect—there is always room for new observations, theories, measurements."[1]

Sir Alan Rudge, a Fellow of the Royal Society and former member of the UK government's Scientific Advisory Committee, told the *Times* (London) that the society had taken an "unnecessarily alarmist position" on man-made climate change.[2] Kenneth Green, an environmental scientist wrote, "Desperation is setting in among climate alarmists who by their own math can see that the window is rapidly closing on 'saving the planet.'"[3]

In light of the growing repudiation of the most outrageous claims of the AGW movement, the public finally has a chance to hear two sides of the issue. Some scientists are beginning to discuss how humanity might adapt to any future global warming, as humans have done in the past. Such an approach takes into account the intelligence, adaptability, and resourcefulness of humans. Some climate scientists now acknowledge that there are workable solutions other than attempting to destroy the West's fossil fuel–based economy and standard of living. The voices of these climate scientists offer an argument against the hidden political agenda of the socialist-globalist elite. Excessive taxes and government regulations, plus treaties and laws mandating debilitating reductions in carbon dioxide (CO_2) emissions, are not designed primarily to save the planet. The globalist elites want nothing less than to install a centralized, global government under the United Nations with power over the democracies of the West.

The IPCC's reputation for integrity and scientific accuracy was seriously compromised following repudiations by former IPCC scientific contributors and revelations of scientific errors and false statements in past IPCC reports. *Newsweek* magazine wrote that "some of the IPCC's most-quoted data and recommendations were taken straight out of unchecked activist brochures, newspaper articles, and corporate reports—including claims of plummeting crop yields in Africa and the rising costs of warming-related natural disasters, both of which have been refuted by academic studies."[4]

Meanwhile, China, India, and other developing nations have refused to sign a treaty designed to reduce their carbon emissions. Those nations began to view the treaty as an economic suicide pact promoted by the West to prevent them from growing their economies to achieve the wealth that the West has already achieved.

THE GLOBAL WARMING PETITION PROJECT

Al Gore and the global-warming alarmists repeatedly claim that the IPCC report that supposedly documented man-made global warming represented a consensus of 2,500 climate scientists. However, a careful analysis of the names on the list reveals a large number of individuals who have no scientific expertise in climate studies or meteorology.

Professor Mike Hulme is a prominent climate scientist and key IPCC insider. He claims that the IPCC seriously misled the news media and the public with its claims that thousands of climate scientists formed a unanimous consensus regarding man-made global warming. Hulme wrote a paper for *Progress in Physical Geography* stating that the actual number of climate scientists who backed that IPCC report's AGW claim was "only a few dozen experts." He added, "Claims such as '2,500 of the world's leading scientists have reached a consensus that human activities are having a significant influence on the climate' are disingenuous."[5]

In contrast, 31,487 American climate scientists—including 9,029 scientists who have PhD's—signed on in support of the Global Warming Petition Project, which declares that the theory of catastrophic global warming is not supported by scientific evidence. The petition also states that CO_2 is a beneficial gas, not a pollutant. Here is the petition's wording:

We urge the United States government to reject the global warming agreement that was written in Kyoto, Japan in December, 1997, and any other similar proposals. The proposed limits on greenhouse gases would harm the environment, hinder the advance of science and technology, and damage the health and welfare of mankind.

There is no convincing scientific evidence that human release of carbon dioxide, methane, or other greenhouse gases is causing or will, in the foreseeable future, cause catastrophic heating of the Earth's atmosphere and disruption of the Earth's climate. Moreover, there is substantial scientific evidence that increases in atmospheric carbon dioxide produce many beneficial effects upon the natural plant and animal environments of the Earth.[6]

AGW PROPONENTS FIGHT BACK

Of course, the powerful political and economic forces behind global-warming alarmism are not planning to close up shop and go home. One new approach that is already being implemented is to refocus the discussion and terminology when sounding the alarm over the looming environmental "threat." The IPCC has transformed the language used in its pronouncements on global-warming issues. The phrase *greenhouse effect* long ago was shifted to *global warming*. Later it was altered in favor of *climate challenge*. Now the preferred term is the more ambiguous *climate science*.

In an attempt to counter the arguments against man-made global warming, some environmental groups, including the World Wildlife Fund (WWF), are helping group members respond to friends who question the AGW campaign. The WWF has placed articles on its Web site, such as "How to Answer the Claims of a Climate Change Sceptic." The article lists standard answers to use in responding to issues raised by critics.[7]

Those who are pushing the socialist-globalist agenda are preparing an additional propaganda campaign to panic people into following their energy-destroying solutions—but this time to also serve the cause of saving the planet's millions of threatened species. The "save the environment" fallback plan is focused on preserving the biodiversity of species throughout the earth from the growing environmental threat of loss of vital habitat. And they argue, of course, that habitats are being destroyed by man-made climate change.

Government delegates from ninety-seven nations met in June 2010 in Busan, South Korea, to prepare to establish a new international environmental body. This international effort will promote the concept that global warming and habitat degradation together will destroy the world as a result of the extinction of numerous species. Delegates plan to put the new "biodiversity crisis" on an equal footing with the purported threat of man-made global warming. They also proposed that the new environmental organization be patterned on the UN IPCC and provisionally be named the Intergovernmental Platform on Biodiversity and Ecosystem Services (IPBES).

An article about the biodiversity planning meeting reported, "The proposed 'IPCC for nature' could provide regular, independent reports on the state of global and regional biodiversity—reflecting the IPCC's five-yearly assessments of the state of climate science, forecasts for impacts and advice about how to tackle the problem."[8] A key proposed IPBES initiative will involve the monitoring of up to 160,000 of the two million known species of insects, marine creatures, birds, reptiles, and animals that scientists have documented.

It's not surprising that globalist leaders would modify their AGW propaganda strategies after nearly twelve years of cooling temperatures (since 1998). The changing climate terminology and their decisions to appeal to the public using a different—but related—"threat" to humanity reveals that the socialist-globalist strategists are undeterred in advancing their hidden agenda. Globalists continue to push ahead in their efforts to radically transform America's free-enterprise economy and eliminate its political independence.

The eco-fundamentalists, radical environmentalists, AGW movement leaders, and now the biodiversity camp care nothing for the fundamental rights and freedoms that are guaranteed in the U.S. Constitution. Unfortunately, the vast majority of citizens are unaware of the global-warming deception and the hidden political agenda to radically transform our economy and our way of life.

It isn't surprising that the AGW camp is divided, with some former supporters calling for unbiased science and others fighting even harder to maintain the movement's hidden agenda. Professor Mojib Latif of the Leibniz Institute of Marine Sciences at Kiel University, Germany, is an author for the IPCC reports. Latif is considered one of the world's top computer modelers to plot future climate change. Latif claimed that we may now be entering a cooling period of up to one or possibly two decades, during which global temperatures will follow a cooling trend despite continuing increases in man-made CO_2 in the atmosphere. He predicted a significant natural cooling trend will occur based on solar radiation trends and cyclical changes to major ocean currents, as well as water temperatures in the North Atlantic, that would dominate over the warming influence caused by human CO_2 contributions. The cooling would be caused by the "Pacific and Atlantic 'multi-decadal oscillations' (MDOs)."[9] At the UN World Climate Conference in Geneva, Switzerland, Latif declared that "people will say this is global warming disappearing." Significantly, a number of climate scientists admitted that, on time scales involving twenty to thirty years, natural climate variability is at least as important to climate projections as the long-term climate changes from man-made carbon dioxide emissions.[10]

Vicky Pope, who is associated with the United Kingdom Met Office (the equivalent of the U.S. National Weather Service) and the Climate Research Unit (CRU) at the University of East Anglia, stated, "In many ways we know more about what will happen in the 2050s than next year."[11] However, Pope's claim is ridiculous. If the scientists who designed computer models to predict climate change failed to forecast the last twelve years of global cooling (and they did), how can we have confidence in their projections that look forty or ninety years into the future? Why would the United States or any other industrialized nation hold back its agriculture, manufacturing, power-generating capacity, and transportation systems based on a computer projection when we know that the projection was blind to twelve years of global cooling?

GOD IS SOVEREIGN OVER THE ENVIRONMENT

Regardless of the lack of reliable, objective scientific evidence to support the AGW movement's claims, those who support the global-warming deception will not retreat from pursuing their hidden agenda. The AGW camp will continue to push their propaganda campaigns, leverage their political influence, and use regulations and treaties to destroy the Western way of life. The AGW camp will fight for biodiversity in the name of protecting all species as they work simultaneously for additional penalties, taxes, laws, and treaties to limit carbon emissions. They have invested their careers, financial resources, and their reputations in the AGW campaign. They won't give up that cause to suddenly work exclusively for the protection of wildlife habitats and endangered species.

The AGW movement will continue to push its restrictive and undemocratic environmental, economic, and political policies in a sustained effort to establish a socialist global dictatorship. As we awaken to the grim results of this struggle—the lies and deception, the confusion, the guilt and fear-mongering—Christians need to be reminded that we are not alone. We have access to God's truth and His Holy Spirit to give us spiritual discernment. While the AGW movement continues to resort to manufactured environmental "crises" to gain political support, the Bible reassures us that the earth's climate is under God's benevolent control. The Scriptures state that God gave humanity dominion over the earth, its resources, and the life that the earth sustains. God told Adam and Eve to rule over creation and subdue it. "And God blessed them, and God said unto them, Be fruitful, and multiply, and replenish the earth, and subdue it: and have dominion over the fish of the sea, and over the fowl of the air, and over every living thing that moveth upon the earth" (Genesis 1:28).

The Lord gave humans a privileged place among all of His millions of creatures. He commanded us to responsibly exercise stewardship over the earth and its creatures. "Thou madest him [man] to have dominion over the works of thy hands; thou hast put all things under his feet: all sheep and oxen, yea, and the beasts of the field; the fowl of the air, and the fish of the sea, and whatsoever passeth through the paths of the seas" (Psalm 8:6–8).

None of this has changed, no matter what we read in the news or hear regarding UN actions and international climate treaties. Our biblically mandated duty of stewardship over the earth requires us to commit ourselves to the responsible caretaking of the environment. As followers of God and His Scriptures, we must never casually abuse the earth's bounty. God's command to us to exercise dominion over the earth means that we are required to intelligently manage all the resources that God has given us. Therefore, we must preserve and protect the earth's resources, especially its atmosphere and water resources.

When we consider the earth and its remarkable qualities, we can see that all the resources that God has provided for humanity's needs are either renewable or practically inexhaustible. The Lord continues to provide sun and rain, as well as the changing seasons necessary to sustain and replenish vital resources. According to the terms and purpose of the law of the sabbath of the land, referred to in the books of Exodus and Leviticus, the Lord commanded that Israel was to give the land a rest, a sabbath, every seven years. Israel's fields and vineyards were to be sown and harvested annually for six years, then the land was to be left fallow during the whole of the seventh year. This practice allowed the soil's nutrients to replenish to guarantee the continued provision of bountiful crops (see Exodus 23:10–11; Leviticus 25:1–7). God promised that He would provide a bumper harvest during every sixth year to supply enough food to cover the seventh, fallow year. This also provided the essential seed stock to replant and resume the growing cycle following the sabbath year.

God's unbreakable promise to humanity after the end of the Flood was His prophecy that He would never end the pattern of variability in temperature and climate. He promised to continue the sequence of seasons that are essential to life on earth. God declared, "While the earth remaineth, seedtime and harvest, and cold and heat, and summer and winter, and day and night shall not cease" (Genesis 8:22). Part of our responsibility in protecting life and being good stewards of the earth is to protect its future against the lies and conspiracies of the man-made global-warming alarmist movement.

HOW WE SHOULD RESPOND TO THE GLOBAL-WARMING DECEPTION

It is my hope that every reader now recognizes the profound, growing danger to our freedoms and liberties. A question that will arise for many concerned readers is this: What can I do to help preserve the free-enterprise market economy that has made North America the envy of billions of people around the world? The first thing we should consider is how to awaken our friends, family, and neighbors to the truth about the global-warming deception. We need to also make people aware of the hidden political agenda of those who plan to transform America into a weakened, economically despoiled, socialist society. Sharing this book with those around you will provide them with an understanding of the real dangers facing all who love their country and our way of life. In addition, the select bibliography at the end of this book suggests several excellent books that will supply additional information and insights into the global-warming deception.

We need to exercise our political responsibility as free citizens by communicating with our senators and representatives by letter or e-mail. Let them know that you oppose any legislative votes to ratify climate-control treaties or to enact taxes, regulations, or restrictive laws that seek to weaken our nation politically or economically. Remember that members of Congress tabulate the written communications they receive from voters. They know that for every voter who sends a letter or an e-mail, there are probably more than one hundred other voters who feel the same way but fail to write. Tell your elected representatives that you want them to defend liberty and our free-enterprise economy. Remind them that your vote in the next election will be strongly influenced by their actions.

Finally, as people who share a strong faith in God, we need to pray daily for His wisdom and guidance for our nation's preservation, for our leaders, and for each family's protection. There is no question that we are living in a time of grave challenge for America. Our personal freedoms and our entire way of life are at stake.

Although the global-warming deception is an unprecedented challenge to our liberties and standard of living, we do not stand alone in facing the challenge. Remember the words of Scripture:

If my people, which are called by my name, shall humble themselves, and pray, and seek my face, and turn from their wicked ways; then will I hear from heaven, and will forgive their sin, and will heal their land. (2 Chronicles 7:14)

NOTES

Chapter 1

1. Herman Van Rompuy, quoted in Daniel Hannan, "Herman Van Rompuy: Today the EU, Tomorrow the World!" *Daily Telegraph* (UK), November 21, 2009, http://blogs.telegraph.co.uk/news/danielhannan/100017487/herman-van-rompuy-today-the-eu-tomorrow-the-world/.

2. Mike Thompson, quoted in Rick Montgomery, "Many Meteorologists Reject Warming Claims," *Virginian-Pilot and the Ledger-Star* (Norfolk, VA), February 23, 2010, http://findarticles.com/p/news-articles/virginian-pilot-ledger-star-norfolk/mi_8014/is_20100223/meteorologists-reject-warming-claims/ai_n50199117/.

3. Quote taken from a speech given by Havel Wolf, in "Socialism and Global Warming," Conservapedia, www.conservapedia.com/Socialism_and_global_warming. See also "Socialism/Communism at Work in America? You Decide," a Freedom Alert insert, January 5, 1998.

4. Warren Meyer, *A Skeptical Layman's Guide to Man-Made Global Warming,* quoted in "Socialism and Global Warming," Conservapedia, October 5, 2010, http://politifi.com/news/Socialism-and-global-warming-1184387.html.

5. Louis Proyect, quoted in "Is Climate Change Really Even an Environmental Issue?" May 25, 2010, http://interventionprograms.info/intervention/4178/is-climate-change-really-even-an-environmental-issue/.

6. Maurice F. Strong, quoted in Judi McLeody, "Glenn Beck: Meet Maurice Strong," *Canada Free Press,* May 13, 2010, www.canadafreepress.com/index.php/article/23141/.

7. Al Gore, *Earth in the Balance* (New York: Houghton Mifflin, 1992), 269, (italics added for emphasis).

8. Christopher Horner, "Leaked Doc Proves Spain's 'Green' Policies—the Basis for Obama's—an Economic Disaster," *Pajamas Media,* May 18, 2010, http://pajamasmedia.com/blog/spains-green-policies-an-economic-disaster/.

9. Carbon Sense Coalition, "The Sky Is Not Falling," January 2008, V3, 13–14, www.co2web.info/Garnaut_Carbon-Sense_0801.pdf.

10. Alexander King and Bertrand Schneider, *The First Global Revolution: A Report by the Council of the Club of Rome* (Hyderabad, India: Orient Longman, 1993), 75 (italics added for emphasis, except in the phrase *human intervention,* where the emphasis is present in the original document).

11. Daniel B. Botkin, "Global Warming Delusions," *Wall Street Journal,* October 17, 2007, http://online.wsj.com/article/NA_WSJ_PUB:SB11 9258265537661384.html.

12. Al Gore, *Earth in the Balance* (New York: Houghton Mifflin, 1992), 274.

13. James Delingpole, "Politics," *Telegraph.co. UK,* October 9, 2010, http:// blogs.telegraph.co.uk/news/jamesdelingpole/100058265/us-physics-professor-global-warming-is-the-greatest-and-most-successful-pseudo scientific-fraud-i-have-seen-in-my-long-life/.

14. Peter Foster, "Denial Not Just for the Deniers," *National Post* (Ontario), February 18, 2010, http://network.nationalpost.com/NP/blogs/full comment/archive/2010/02/18/peter-foster-denial-not-just-for-the-deniers. aspx#ixzz0g74isAF8/.

15. Kiminori Itoh, quoted in Marc Morano, "Ignorant Skeptics?: UN Scientist Prof. Trenberth Says Only 'Poorly Informed' Scientists Disagree with UN—Appeals to Authority: 'The IPCC Has Spoken,'" Climate Depot, October 13, 2009, www.climatedepot.com/a/3308/Ignorant-Skeptics-UN-Scientist-Prof-Trenberth-says-only-poorly-informed-scientists-disagree-with-UN--Appeals-to-Authority-The-IPCC-has-spoken/.

Chapter 2

1. Václav Klaus and Fred L. Smith Jr., *Blue Planet in Green Shackles* (Washington, D.C.: Competitive Enterprise Institute, 2008), 85, (italics added).

2. Klaus and Smith, *Blue Planet in Green Shackles,* 82.

3. H. L. Mencken, *In Defense of Women* (Whitefish, MT: Kessinger, 1918), section 2, chapter 13.

4. William Soon, quoted in J. Blethen, "Soon: Alarmists Have Captured the Scientific Paper Process," Heliogenic Climate Change, March 11, 2009, www.heliogenic.net/2009/03/11/soon-alarmists-have-captured-the-scientific-paper-process/.

5. E. Beck, "180 Years of Atmospheric CO_2 Gas Analysis by Chemical Methods," *Energy and Environment* 18: 2007, 259–82, www.friends ofscience.org/assets/files/documents/CO2 Gas Analysis-Ernst-Georg Beck.pdf.

6. For more on methods of measuring carbon dioxide levels in the atmosphere, see Ian Plimer, *Heaven and Earth* (Lanham, MD: Taylor Trade, 2009), 416.

7. William Kininmonth, quoted in "Climate Change Is Natural: 100 Reasons Why," *Daily Express* (UK), December 15, 2009, www.dailyexpress.co.uk/posts/view/146138.

8. For more on this, see Plimer, *Heaven and Earth,* 144.

9. For more on this, see David Whitehouse, "Has Global Warming Stopped?" *New Statesman,* December 19, 2007, www.newstatesman.com/scitech/2007/12/global-warming-temperature/.

10. S. Solomon, D. Qin, M. Manning, Z. Chen, M. Marquis, K. B. Averyt, M. Tignor, and H. L. Miller, eds., *Climate Change 2007: The Physical Science Basis (Contribution of Working Group I to the Fourth Assessment Report of the Intergovernmental Panel on Climate Change, 2007),* "Summary for Policymakers" (Cambridge, UK: Cambridge University Press, 2007), 5, www.ipcc.ch/pdf/assessment-report/ar4/wg1/ar4-wg1-spm.pdf.

11. S. Solomon et al., *Climate Change 2007: The Physical Science Basis,* 10.

12. Roy Spencer, "Warming in Last 50 Years Predicted by Natural Climate Cycles," June 6, 2010, www.drroyspencer.com/2010/06/warming-in-last-50-years-predicted-by-natural-climate-cycles/.

13. Bjorn Lomborg, *Cool It* (New York: Alfred A. Knopf, 2007), 16.

Chapter 3

1. John Bellamy Foster, "The End of Rational Capitalism," *Monthly Review* 56, no. 10 (March 2005), http://www.monthlyreview.org/0305jbf.htm.

2. Michael G. Fullan, "The Professional Teacher—Why Teachers Must Become Change Agents," *Educational Leadership* 50, no. 6 (March 1993): 1, www.csus.edu/indiv/j/jelinekd/EDTE 227/Fullen change.pdf.

3. Karl Marx and Friedrich Engels, *The Communist Manifesto* (Oxford: Oxford World Classics, 2008), chap. 2.

4. Gus Hall, quoted in "Socialism and Global Warming," Conservapedia, www.conservapedia.com/Socialism_and_global_warming.

5. Maurice King, quoted in The Green Agenda, www.green-agenda.com/neweconomy.html.

6. Maurice Strong, "Economic Growth Is Not the Cure; It Is the Disease," *Edmonton Journal,* July 18, 2003, A18.

7. Carroll Quigley, *Tragedy and Hope* (New York: Macmillan, 1966), 278.

8. Al Gore, "On Katrina, Global Warming" (speech, National Sierra Club convention, San Francisco, CA, September 9, 2005), quoted in Common Dreams, September 12, 2005, www.commondreams.org/views05/0912-32.htm.

9. Strong, "Economic Growth Is Not the Cure."

10. Peter Foster, "Denial Not Just for the Deniers," *National Post* (Ontario), February 18, 2010, http://network.nationalpost.com/NP/blogs/full comment/archive/2010/02/18/peter-foster-denial-not-just-for-the-deniers. aspx#ixzz0g7BsG9gJ/.

11. Joseph L. Bast, "Eight Reasons Why 'Global Warming' Is a Scam," Heartland Institute, February 2003, www.heartland.org/policybot/results/11548/February_2003_Eight_Reasons_Why_Global_Warming_Is_a_Scam. html/.

12. Gro Harlem Brundtland, quoted in Warren Meyer, *Is It OK to Be a Skeptic?* (Chap. 2, "Skeptics Guide to Global Warming"), Climate Skeptic, September 6, 2007, www.climate-skeptic.com/2007/09/chapter-2-skept.html/.

13. Steve Connor, "C4 Accused of Falsifying Data in Documentary on Climate

Change," *Independent* (UK), May 8, 2007, www.independent.co.uk/news/
media/c4-accused-of-falsifying-data-in-documentary-on-climate-change-
447927.html/.

14. Richard A. Kerr, "Climate Change: Greenhouse Forecasting Still Cloudy,"
Science 276, no. 5315 (May 16, 1997): 1040–42, www.sciencemag.org/cgi/
content/full/sci;276/5315/1040/.

15. Chris Folland, quoted in Stephen Tonkin, "Computer Model Limitations,"
www.astunit.com/crocodiles/models.htm (brackets in the original).

16. For more on this, see Michael Hudson, *Global Fracture: The New International Economic Order* (New York: Harper & Row, 1977).

17. Ross Gelbspan, quoted in Kenneth P. Green, "The New Dissidents,"
American: The Journal of the Enterprise Institute, April 17, 2008, www.
american.com/archive/2008/april-04-08/the-new-dissidents.

18. Barack Obama, "Energy Independence and the Safety of Our Planet," April
3, 2006, http://obamaspeeches.com/060-Energy-Independence-and-the-
Safety-of-Our-Planet-Obama-Speech.htm.

19. John Holdren, Anne Ehrlich, and Paul Ehrlich, *Human Ecology: Problems
and Solutions* (San Francisco: W. H. Freeman, 1973), 279.

20. Michael Oppenheimer, quoted in Jon Basil Utley, "Why the Global
Warming Hoax?" *American Conservative,* December 12, 2009, www.
amconmag.com/blog/2009/12/12/why-the-global-warming-hoax/.

21. Jan Tinbergen, "Global Governance for the 21st Century," Special Contribution in UN *Human Development Report 1994* (New York: Oxford
University Press, 1994), 88, http://hdr.undp.org/en/media/hdr_1994_en_
chap4.pdf.

Chapter 4

1. Jay Leno, *The Tonight Show,* NBC, February 3, 2009.

2. Sir John Houghton, quoted in Dr. Tim Ball, "How UN Structures Were
Designed to Prove Human CO_2 Was Causing Global Warming," *Canada
Free Press,* April 30, 2008, www.canadafreepress.com/index.php/
article/2840.

3. Paul Watson, Dixy Lee Ray, and Lou Guzzo, *Environmental Overkill* (New York: Perennial, 1993), 172.

4. Christine Stewart, quoted in Terrence Corcoran, "Global Warming: The Real Agenda," *Financial Post* (Canada), December 26, 1998, brackets in the original, www.sepp.org/Archive/reality/realagenda.html.

5. Timothy Wirth, quoted in Michael Fumento, *Science Under Siege* (New York: William Morrow, 1993), 362.

6. "Geologists Think the World May Be Frozen Up Again," *New York Times,* February 24, 1895.

7. "Prof. Schmidt Warns Us of an Encroaching Ice Age," *Times* (London), October 7, 1912.

8. "Scientists Say Arctic Ice Will Wipe Out Canada," *Chicago Tribune,* August 9, 1923.

9. "Science: Another Ice Age?" *Time,* June 24, 1974, www.time.com/time/magazine/article/0,9171,944914-1,00.html#ixzz0xKMX368o/.

10. Significantly, one of the major voices announcing the "global cooling" crisis in the 1970s was John Holdren, now President Barack Obama's science czar. Isn't it odd that today, Holdren is one of the great proponents of man-made global *warming*? You might have heard the maxim "Don't let a crisis go to waste." In other words, any crisis will do, it doesn't matter whether it is genuine. There are left-wing political forces that make full use of fear tactics to try to ramrod their socialist-Marxist policies through Congress.

11. Kenneth E. F. Watt (speech, Swarthmore College, first Earth Day, April 22, 1970), www.swarthmore.edu/x29477.xml.

12. Paul Ehrlich, quoted in Mike Austin, "Eco-Madness," Diary and Commentary, 14, http://mikeaustin.org/diary_and_commentary14.htm.

13. Austin, "Eco-Madness."

14. *Science News,* March 1, 1975, cover illustration.

15. Bonner R. Cohen, "EPA's Dredging Scheme Will Wreak Havoc on the Hudson River," *Human Events,* January 7, 2002, http://findarticles.com/p/articles/mi_qa3827/is_200201/ai_n9034723/.

16. Renate D. Kimbrough, Martha L. Doemland, and Maurice E. LeVois,

"Mortality in Male and Female Capacitor Workers Exposed to Polychlori-nated Biphenyls," *Journal of Occupational and Environmental Medicine* 41, no. 3 (March 1999): 161–71, http://journals.lww.com/joem/Abstract/1999/03000/Mortality_in_Male_and_Female_Capacitor_Workers.5.aspx.

17. Robert Gwadz, quoted in Michael Finkel, "Malaria," *National Geographic,* July 2007, http://ngm.nationalgeographic.com/2007/07/malaria/finkel-text/8.

18. Nicholas D. Kristof, "It's Time to Spray DDT," *New York Times,* January 8, 2005, www.nytimes.com/2005/01/08/opinion/8kristof.html.

19. For more on this idea, see John Tierney, "Fateful Voice of a Generation Still Drowns Out Real Science," *New York Times,* June 5, 2007, www.nytimes.com/2007/06/05/science/earth/05tier.html/.

20. James M. Inhofe, "The Science of Climate Change" (Senate floor state-ment, July 28, 2003), http://inhofe.senate.gov/pressreleases/climate.htm.

21. Ian Plimer, *Heaven and Earth* (Lanham, MD: Taylor Trade, 2009), 165.

22. For more on this, see Manfred Mudelsee, "The Phase Relations Among Atmospheric CO_2 Content, Temperature and Global Ice Volume over the Past 420 ka," *Quarternary Science Reviews* 20 (2001), 583–89, www.manfredmudelsee.com/publ/pdf/The_phase_relations_among_atmospheric_CO2_content_temperature_and_global_ice_volume_over_the_past_420_ka.pdf.

23. Plimer, *Heaven and Earth,* 115.

24. Plimer, *Heaven and Earth,* 115.

25. For more on this, see "Climate Change Is Natural: 100 Reasons Why," *Daily Express* (UK), December 15, 2009, www.dailyexpress.co.uk/posts/view/146138/.

26. David Deming, "Climate Change and the Media" (speech, U.S. Senate Committee on Environment and Public Works, December 6, 2006), http://epw.senate.gov/hearing_statements.cfm?id=266543. Also www.openmarket.org/wp.../climate-change-reconsidered-heat-islands.pdf.

27. Scientists form estimates of increases in future global temperature based on mathematical projections from computer models. The computer models

have been developed primarily at two institutions: the Climate Research Unit (CRU) at the University of East Anglia in the United Kingdom and the Goddard Institute for Space Studies (GISS) at Columbia University in New York.

28. Plimer, *Heaven and Earth*, 99.

Chapter 5

1. Ian Plimer, *Heaven and Earth* (Lanham, MD: Taylor Trade, 2009), 109.
2. Plimer, *Heaven and Earth*, 99.
3. Plimer, *Heaven and Earth*, 115.
4. Plimer, *Heaven and Earth*, 115.
5. "Climate Change Is Natural: 100 Reasons Why," *Daily Express* (UK), December 15, 2009, www.dailyexpress.co.uk/posts/view/146138/.
6. Marc Morano, "Inhofe Debunks So-Called 'Consensus' on Global Warming," October 26, 2007, http://epw.senate.gov/public/index.cfm?FuseAction=Minority.Blogs&ContentRecord_id=595F6F41-802A-23AD-4BC4-B364B623ADA3/.
7. Christopher C. Horner, *Red Hot Lies* (Washington, D.C.: Regnery, 2006), 148–53.
8. Finnegan admitted on Irish Radio, during a debate with documentary filmmaker Phelim McAleer, that he had not read the full report. See Kristin McMurray, "IPCC Member Admits to Not Reading IPCC Report," Scribd, February 24, 2010, www.scribd.com/doc/30424025/IPCC-Member-Admits-to-Not-Reading-IPCC-Report/.
9. Ján Veizer, Yves Godderis, and Louis M. François, "Evidence for Decoupling of Atmospheric CO_2 and Global Climate During the Phanerozoic Eon," *Nature* 408, no. 6813 (December 7, 2000): 698–701, www.nature.com/nature/journal/v408/n6813/abs/408698a0.html.
10. Plimer, *Heaven and Earth*, 438–39.
11. Steven M. Japar, quoted in Marc Morano, "Ignorant Skeptics?: UN Scientist Prof. Trenberth Says Only 'Poorly Informed' Scientists Disagree with UN—Appeals to Authority: 'The IPCC Has Spoken,'" Climate

Depot, October 13, 2009 (brackets in the original), www.climatedepot. com/a/3308/Ignorant-Skeptics-UN-Scientist-Prof-Trenberth-says-only-poorly-informed-scientists-disagree-with-UN--Appeals-to-Authority-The-IPCC-has-spoken/.

12. Vincent Gray, quoted in Morano, "Ignorant Skeptics?"

13. John Brignell, quoted in Morano, "Ignorant Skeptics?"

14. John McLean, quoted in Morano, "Ignorant Skeptics?"

15. Philip Lloyd, quoted in Morano, "Ignorant Skeptics?"

16. Madhav Khandekar, quoted in Morano, "Ignorant Skeptics?" (brackets in the original).

17. Christopher W. Landsea, quoted in Morano, "Ignorant Skeptics?" (brackets in the original).

18. Frederick Seitz, "A Major Deception on Global Warming," *Wall Street Journal,* June 12, 1996 (brackets in the original), www.sepp.org/Archive/controv/ipcccont/Item05.htm.

19. Roger Pielke Sr., quoted in Morano, "Ignorant Skeptics?" (brackets in the original).

20. Andreas Fischlin and Guy F. Midgley, *Climate Change 2007: Impacts, Adaptation and Vulnerability (Contribution of Working Group II to the Fourth Assessment Report of the Intergovernmental Panel on Climate Change),* "Ecosystems, Their Properties, Goods and Services" (Cambridge, UK: Cambridge University Press, 2007), 213, www.ipcc.ch/pdf/assessment-report/ar4/wg2/ar4-wg2-chapter4.pdf.

21. Intergovernmental Panel on Climate Change, 13.4.1 Natural Ecosystems, http://www.ipcc.ch/publications_and_data/ar4/wg2/en/ch13s13-4. html#13-4-1. See also Andy Rowell and Peter F. Moore, "Global Review of Forest Fires," WWF/IUCN, Gland, Switzerland, 66, http://data.iucn.org/dbtw-wpd/edocs/2000-047.pdf.

Chapter 6

1. "Al Gore—Generation Investment Management," Stockpickr, http://stockpickr.com/port/Al-Gore-Generation-Investment-Management/.

2. Ian Plimer, *Heaven and Earth* (Lanham, MD: Taylor Trade, 2009), 486.

3. Al Gore, interview by Leslie Stahl, *60 Minutes,* CBS, March 30, 2008, www.cbsnews.com/stories/2008/03/27/60minutes/main3974389_page4 .shtml?tag=contentMain;contentBody.

4. Al Gore, *An Inconvenient Truth* (New York: Rodale, 2006), 196–209. In contrast, historical records on temperature trends do not bear out his claim. See "Pre-Industrial Atmospheric CO_2 and Proxy Air and Sea Surface Temperature Data Provide No Evidence," Center for Science and Public Policy and Center for the Study of Carbon Dioxide and Global Change, January 4, 2007, http://ff.org/centers/csspp/pdf/20070204_ idso.pdf.

5. Louise Gray, "England Is Sinking While Scotland Rises Above Sea Levels, According to New Study," *Telegraph* (UK), October 7, 2009, www. telegraph.co.uk/earth/earthnews/6226537/England-is-sinking-while-Scotland-rises-above-sea-levels-according-to-new-study.html.

6. R. K. Pachauri and A. Reisinger, eds., *Climate Change 2007: Synthesis Report. Contribution of Working Groups I, II and III to the Fourth Assessment Report of the Intergovernmental Panel on Climate Change* (Geneva: IPCC, 2007), www.ipcc.ch/pdf/assessment-report/ar4/syr/ar4_syr.pdf. See also www.ipcc.ch/publications_and_data/publications_ipcc_fourth_ assessment_report_wg1_report_the_physical_science_basis.htm.

7. Pachauri and Reisinger, *Climate Change 2007: Synthesis Report,* Table 3.1 (p. 45), also on p. 47, www.ipcc.ch/pdf/assessment-report/ar4/syr/ar4_ syr.pdf.

8. Anthony Watts, "Arctic Sea Ice Melt Appears to Have Turned the Corner for 2009," September 15, 2009, http://wattsupwiththat. com/2009/09/15/arctic-sea-ice-melt-appears-to-have-turned-the-corner-for-2009/.

9. Gore, *An Inconvenient Truth* (book) 146–47.

10. "Where Are All the Drowning Polar Bears?" *World Climate Report,* May

16, 2008, www.worldclimatereport.com/index.php/2008/05/16/where-are-all-the-drowning-polar-bears/.

11. U.S. Fisheries and Wildlife Service, Report April 6, 2006.

12. Plimer, *Heaven and Earth,* 199.

13. Leslie Allen, "Will Tuvalu Disappear Beneath the Sea?" *Smithsonian,* August 2004, www.smithsonianmag.com/travel/tuvalu.html?c=y&page=1.

14. Nils-Axel Mörner, quoted in Christopher Booker, "Rise in Sea Levels Is 'the Greatest Lie Ever Told,'" *Telegraph* (UK), March 28, 2009 (parentheses in the original), www.telegraph.co.uk/comment/columnists/christopherbooker/5067351/Rise-of-sea-levels-is-the-greatest-lie-ever-told.html.

15. Booker, "Rise in Sea Levels."

16. *An Inconvenient Truth* (PowerPoint), directed by Davis Guggenheim, Paramount, 2006.

17. John O'Sullivan, "Oceangate: Sea Level Proven to Have Fallen for Past Six Years," Climategate, February 17, 2010, www.climategate.com/sea-levels-proven-to-have-fallen-for-past-six-years.

18. O'Sullivan, "Oceangate."

19. Gore, *An Inconvenient Truth* (book), 42–47.

20. George Landrith, "High Court: Gore's Movie Is One-Sided, Alarmist, and Exaggerated," Frontiers of Freedom, October 11, 2007, www.ff.org/centers/csspp/pdf/KilimanMAC4804.pdf/index.php?option=com_content&task=view&id=386&Itemid=67/.

21. Gore, *An Inconvenient Truth* (book), 58.

22. Gore, *An Inconvenient Truth* (book), 58–61.

23. Margaret Munro, "Frozen in Time: Error on Himalayan Glaciers Melts UN Climate Panel's Reputation," ICECAP, June 10, 2010, http://icecap.us/index.php/go/new-and-cool/error_on_himalayan_glaciers_melts_un_climate_panels_reputation/.

24. Gore, *An Inconvenient Truth* (book), 116–19.

25. Christopher Monckton, "35 Inconvenient Truths: The Errors in Al Gore's Movie," Science and Public Policy Institute, October 19, 2007, http://scienceandpublicpolicy.org/monckton/goreerrors.html.

26. Monckton, "35 Inconvenient Truths."

27. Josefino C. Comiso, "2000: Variability and Trends in Antarctic Surface Temperatures from In Situ and Satellite Infrared Measurements," *Journal of Climate* 13, no. 10 (May 2000): 1674–96, http://journals.ametsoc.org/doi/abs/10.1175/1520-0442(2000)013<1674%3AVATIAS >2.0.CO%3B2.

28. Curt H. Davis, Yonghong Li, Joseph R. McConnell, Markus M. Frey, and Edward Hanna, "Snowfall-Driven Growth in East Antarctic Ice Sheet Mitigates Recent Sea-Level Rise," *Science* 308, no. 5730 (June 24, 2005): 1898–1901, www.sciencemag.org/cgi/content/short/308/5730/1898.

29. *Encyclopedia Britannica Online,* s.v. "Greenland Ice Sheet."

30. David Lambert, *Field Guide to Geology* (New York: Diagram Visual, 1988), 154.

31. Comiso, "2000: Variability and Trends in Antarctic Surface Temperatures." See also http://icecap.us/.../Ice_Core_Sites_In_Greenland_Show_Snow_Levels_Rising.pdf –.

32. Monckton, "35 Inconvenient Truths."

33. "Chilly February Caps Coldest Winter in Three Decades over South Florida," National Weather Service, Weather Forecast Office, Miami, FL, February 2010, www.srh.noaa.gov/images/mfl/news/Feb2010Winter Summary.pdf.

34. "Chilly February Caps Coldest Winter in Three Decades over South Florida," NOAA, National Weather Service, Weather Forecast Office, Miami, FL, February 2010, www.srh.noaa.gov/images/mfl/news/Feb2010 WinterSummary.pdf.

35. Fiona MacRae, "Coldest Winter for More than 30 Years…but Met Office Defends Its Long Range Forecast," *Daily Mail* (UK), March 2, 2010, www.dailymail.co.uk/news/article-1254675/Weather.html.

36. Al Gore, "We Can't Wish Away Climate Change," *New York Times*, February 28, 2010, www.nytimes.com/2010/02/28/opinion/28gore.html?pagewanted=all/.

37. Gore, *An Inconvenient Truth* (book), 100–113.

38. CO_2 Science, "Tornados—Summary," www.co2science.org/subject/t/summaries/tornado.php/.

39. Gore, *An Inconvenient Truth* (book), 84–89.

40. CO_2 Science, "Tornados—Summary."

41. Gore, *An Inconvenient Truth* (book), 100–113.

42. CO_2 Science, "Tornados—Summary."

43. Roger Edwards, Online Tornado FAQ, December 31, 2009, www.spc.noaa.gov/faq/tornado/.

44. Gore, *An Inconvenient Truth* (book), 116–19. See also Monckton, "35 Inconvenient Truths."

45. Monckton, "35 Inconvenient Truths."

46. Paul MacRae, "We're a Long Way from Global-Warming 'Oblivion,'" False Alarm, June 3, 2008, www.paulmacrae.com/?p=29#more-29. Consider this also: "For the majority of greenhouse crops, net photosynthesis increases as CO_2 levels increase from 340–1,000 ppm (parts per million). Most crops show that for any given level of photosynthetically active radiation (PAR), increasing the CO_2 level to 1,000 ppm will increase the photosynthesis by about 50% over ambient CO_2 levels." T. J. Blom, W. A. Straver, F. J. Ingratta, Shalin Khosla, and Wayne Brown, "Carbon Dioxide in Greenhouses," Ministry of Agriculture Food & Rural Affairs, December 2002, www.omafra.gov.on.ca/english/crops/facts/00-077.htm#intro/.

47. Al Gore, interview by Conan O'Brien, *The Tonight Show*, NBC, November 12, 2009.

48. Al Gore, interview by Conan O'Brien, *The Tonight Show*, NBC, November 12, 2009.

49. Al Gore, interview by Conan O'Brien, *The Tonight Show*, NBC, November 12, 2009.

Chapter 7

1. The CRU is one of only three major climate centers charged by the United Nations Intergovernmental Panel on Climate Change (IPCC) with gathering and analyzing climate data. The other two centers are the Goddard Institute for Space Studies (GISS, part of NASA) and the National Oceanographic and Atmospheric Administration (NOAA). These three centers are also charged with analyzing future global climate trends based on sophisticated supercomputer climate models and projections.

2. Steven F. Hayward, "In Denial," The Weekly Standard, American Enterprise Institute for Public Policy Research, March 15, 2010, www.aei.org/article/101757.

3. Ironically, the UK's Meteorological Office in Exeter, Devon, revealed that the office's new £30-million supercomputer, designed to predict future climate change, is itself one of the worst polluters in Britain. The supercomputer, the most powerful computer ever created in the UK, has a staggering fifteen million megabytes of memory and is able to complete a trillion calculations per second. However, it utilizes 1.2 megawatts of energy to run. This is enough energy to power more than one thousand homes. See "Weather Supercomputer Used to Predict Climate Change Is One of Britain's Worst Polluters," Daily Mail (UK), August 27, 2009, www.dailymail.co.uk/sciencetech/article-1209430/Weather-supercomputer-used-predict-climate-change-Britains-worst-polluters.html#ixzz0g7TJS1bK/.

4. Stephen McIntyre and Ross McKitrick, "Corrections to the Mann et. al. (1998) Proxy Data Base and Northern Hemispheric Average Temperature Series," Energy and Environment 14, no. 6 (November 2003): 751–77, http://multi-science.metapress.com/content/r27321306377t46n/?p=a65648 276f294734be359a6f8762a92f&pi=2/.

5. "East Anglia Confirmed Emails from the Climate Research Unit," http://eastangliaemails.com/emails.php?page=4&pp=100.

6. Raymond Bradley, quoted in Rich Trzupek, "The Heretics: McIntyre and McKitrick," FrontPageMag, February 19, 2010, http://frontpagemag.com/2010/02/19/the-heretics-mcintyre-and-mckitrick/.

7. Ian Plimer, *Heaven and Earth* (Lanham, MD: Taylor Trade, 2009), 99.

8. David Deming, "Climate Change and the Media" (statement, U.S. Senate Committee on Environment and Public Works, December 6, 2006), http://epw.senate.gov/hearing_statements.cfm?id=266543.

9. E-mail from Phil Jones to Michael Mann, sent February 2, 2003, "East Anglia Confirmed Emails from the Climate Research Unit—1107454306. txt," www.eastangliaemails.com/emails.php?eid=490&filename=110745 4306.txt/. See also Muir Russell, Geoffrey Boulton, Peter Clarke, David Eyton, and James Norton, *The Independent Climate Change E-Mails Review,* July 2010, www.cce-review.org/pdf/FINAL REPORT.pdf.

10. "'Consensus' Exposed: The CRU Controversy," Minority Staff, United States Senate Committee on Environment and Public Works (Washington, D.C.: Government Printing Office, February 25, 2010), 1, http://epw .senate. gov/public/index.cfm?FuseAction=Files.View&FileStore_id=7db3 fbd8-f1b4-4fdf-bd15-12b7df1a0b63/.

11. Jim Inhofe, quoted in "Senate EPW Minority Releases Report on CRU Controversy," U.S. Senate Committee on Environment and Public Works, February 23, 2010, http://epw.senate.gov/public/index. cfm?FuseAction=Minority.PressReleases&ContentRecord_id=fb6d4083- 802a-23ad-46e8-c5c098e22aa1&Region_id=&Issue_id/.

12. Phil Jones, quoted in Jonathan Petre, "Climategate U-Turn as Scientist at Centre of Row Admits: There Has Been No Global Warming Since 1995," *Daily Mail* (UK), February 14, 2010, www.dailymail.co.uk/news/article- 1250872/Climategate-U-turn-Astonishment-scientist-centre-global- warming-email-row-admits-data-organised.html.

13. Stephen Schneider, quoted in Jonathan Schell, "Our Fragile Earth," *Discover* magazine, October 1989, 47.

14. E-mail from Phil Jones to Michael Mann, May 29, 2008, "East Anglia Confirmed Emails from the Climate Research Unit–1212073451.txt," www.eastangliaemails.com/emails.php?eid=893&filename=.txt/.

15. E-mail from Michael Mann to Tim Osborn, July 31, 2003, "East Anglia Confirmed Emails from the Climate Research Unit–1059664704.txt,"

www.eastangliaemails.com/emails.php?eid=345&filename=105966
4704.txt/.

16. E-mail from Tom Wigley to Phil Jones, October 5, 2007, "East Anglia
Confirmed Emails from the Climate Research Unit–1254756944.txt," www.
eastangliaemails.com/emails.php?eid=1039&filename=1254756944.txt/.

17. Christopher Booker, "Climate Change: This Is the Worst Scientific Scandal
of Our Generation," *Telegraph* (UK), November 28, 2009, www.telegraph.
co.uk/comment/columnists/christopherbooker/6679082/Climate-change-
this-is-the-worst-scientific-scandal-of-our-generation.html.

18. Warwick Hughes, quoted in Patrick J. Michaels, "The Dog Ate Global
Warming," *National Review Online,* September 23, 2009, http://article.
nationalreview.com/407512/the-dog-ate-global-warming/patrick-j-michaels/.

19. Petre, "Climategate U-Turn."

20. Steven McIntyre and Ross McKitrick, "The M&M Project: Replication
Analysis of the Mann et al. Hockey Stick," www.uoguelph.ca/~rmckitri/
research/trc.html.

21. Joseph D'Aleo and Anthony Watts, "Surface Temperature Records: Policy
Driven Deception?" updated June 2, 2010, http://scienceandpublicpolicy.
org/originals/policy_driven_deception.html/.

22. "13 Years of Climategate Emails Show Tawdry Manipulation of Science by
a Powerful Cabal at the Heart of the Global Warming Campaign," January
15, 2010, http://poneke.wordpress.com/2010/01/15/gate/.

23. For more on this, see a detailed analysis of the CRU e-mails conducted by
Christopher Booker in his excellent book, *The Real Global Warming
Disaster: Is the Obsession with "Climate Change" Turning Out to Be the Most
Costly Scientific Blunder in History?* (New York: Continuum, 2009).

24. Petre, "Climategate U-Turn," (italics added).

Chapter 8

1. For more on this, see Ken Gregory, "Climate Change Science," Friends of
Science, August 16, 2010, www.friendsofscience.org/assets/documents/FOS
Essay/Climate_Change_Science.html.

2. Ian Plimer, *Heaven and Earth* (Lanham, MD: Taylor Trade, 2009), 120–31.

3. Lawrence Solomon, "It's the Sun, Stupid," *National Post* (Ontario), May 22, 2010, http://opinion.financialpost.com/2010/05/21/it's-the-sun-stupid/.

4. Richard A. Lovett, "Ebbing Sunspot Activity Makes Europe Freeze," *Nature News,* April 14, 2010, www.nature.com/news/2010/100414/full/news.2010.184.html.

5. Mike Lockwood, quoted in Solomon, "It's the Sun, Stupid."

6. Henrik Svensmark, quoted in Solomon, "It's the Sun, Stupid."

7. William P. Patterson, Kristin A. Dietrich, Chris Holmden, and John T. Andrews, "Two Millennia of North Atlantic Seasonality and Implications for Norse Colonies," *Proceedings of the National Academy of Sciences of the United States of America* 107, no. 12 (March 23, 2010): 5306–10, www.ncbi.nlm.nih.gov/pmc/articles/PMC2851789/.

8. Nicola Scafetta and Bruce J. West, "Estimated Solar Contribution to the Global Surface Warming Using the ACRIM TSI Satellite Composite," *Geophysical Research Letters* 32, no. 24 (September 29, 2005), L18713, doi:10.1029/2005GL023849.

9. Bruce West, "Dr Bruce J. West on Solar Energy Modeling," June 6, 2008, http://globalwarming-arclein.blogspot.com/2008/06/dr-bruce-j-west-on-solar-energy.html.

10. Nicola Scafetta and Bruce J. West, "Phenomenological Solar Contribution to the 1900–2000 Global Surface Warming," *Geophysical Research Letters* 33 (March 9, 2006): L05708, doi:10.1029/2005GL025539, www.agu.org/journals/ABS/2006/2005GL025539.shtml.

11. Habibullo Abdussamatov, quoted in Kate Ravilious, "Mars Melt Hints at Solar, Not Human, Cause for Warming, Scientist Says," National Geographic News, February 28, 2007, http://news.nationalgeographic.com/news/2007/02/070228-mars-warming.html.

12. "Global Warming Hits Mars Too: Study," Breitbart, April 4, 2010, www.breitbart.com/article.php?id=070404203258.5klhwqs4&show_article=.

13. Philip S. Marcus, "Prediction of Global Climate Change on Jupiter," *Nature*

428, no. 6985 (April 22, 2004): 828–31, www.me.berkeley.edu/cfd/people/
marcus/nature02470.pdf.

14. Richard A. Lovett, "Ebbing Sunspot Activity Makes Europe Freeze,"
Naturenews, April 14, 2010, www.nature.com/news/2010/100414/full/
news.2010.184.html.

15. Tony Phillips, "Deep Solar Minimum," Science@NASA, April 5, 2010,
http://science.nasa.gov/science-news/science-at-nasa/2009/01apr_
deepsolarminimum/.

16. Yid with Lid, "Blame the Sun for Global Warming," *The Lid,* December
13, 2009, http://yidwithlid.blogspot.com/2009/12/blame-sun-for-global-
warming.html, (italics added).

17. Plimer, *Heaven and Earth,* 112.

18. Plimer, *Heaven and Earth,* 194.

19. Plimer, *Heaven and Earth,* 165.

20. "Climate Change Is Natural: 100 Reasons Why," *Daily Express* (UK),
December 15, 2009, www.dailyexpress.co.uk/posts/view/146138/.

21. "Climate Change Is Natural: 100 Reasons Why."

22. Brian Sussman, *Climategate* (Washington, D.C.: WND Books,
2010), 67.

23. Sussman, *Climategate,* 67.

24. Sussman, *Climategate,* 70–71.

25. Sussman, *Climategate,* 60–61.

26. Sussman, *Climategate,* 61.

27. Anythony Watts, "Another Global Temp Index Dives in Jan08, this time
HadCRUT," February 19, 2008, Watts Up With That, http://wattsup
withthat.com/2008/02/19/another-global-temp-index-dives-in-jan08-
this-time-hadcrut/.

28. "Climate Change Is Natural: 100 Reasons Why."

29. "Rising CO_2 Boosts Plant Water Use Efficiency," www.plantsneedco2.org/
default.aspx?menuitemid=329&AspxAutoDetectCookieSupport=1/.

30. Sussman, *Climategate,* 69.

Chapter 9

1. Daniel Hannan, "Herman Van Rompuy: Today the EU, Tomorrow the World!" *Telegraph* (UK), November 21, 2009, http://blogs.telegraph.co.uk/news/danielhannan/100017487/herman-van-rompuy-today-the-eu-tomorrow-the-world/.

2. Dominic Lawson, "Kyoto Is Worthless (and You Don't Have to Be a Sceptic to Believe That Now," *Independent* (UK), December 9, 2008, www.independent.co.uk/opinion/commentators/dominic-lawson/dominic-lawson-kyoto-is-worthless-and-you-dont-have-to-be-a-sceptic-to-believe-that-now-1058032.html.

3. Sujata Gupta and Dennis A. Tirpak, *Climate Change 2007: Mitigation of Climate Change (Contribution of Working Group III to the Fourth Assessment Report of the Intergovernmental Panel on Climate Change, 2007),* "Policies, Instruments, and Co-Operative Arrangements" (Cambridge, UK: Cambridge University Press, 2007), 776 (Box 13.7), www.ipcc.ch/pdf/assessment-report/ar4/wg3/ar4-wg3-chapter13.pdf.

4. Andre Illarionov, "Russian Scientists Reassert Opposition to Kyoto Accord," Heartland Institute, September 2004, www.heartland.org/policybot/results/15556/Russian_Scientists_Reassert_Opposition_to_Kyoto_Accord.html/.

5. *Byrd-Hagel Resolution,* S. Res. 98, 105th Congress, 1st sess., www.nationalcenter.org/KyotoSenate.html.

6. Joss Garman, "Copenhagen—Historic Failure That Will Live in Infamy," *Independent* (UK), December 20, 2009, www.independent.co.uk/opinion/commentators/joss-garman-copenhagen--historic-failure-that-will-live-in-infamy-1845907.html.

7. Bjorn Lomborg, *Cool It* (New York: Alfred A. Knopf, 2007), 42, 162.

8. Lomborg, *Cool It,* 42, 162.

9. Lomborg, *Cool It,* 110–12.

10. James Kanter, "New Plans Try to Revive Carbon Trading," *New York Times,* May 24, 2010, www.nytimes.com/2010/05/25/business/global/25carbon.html/.

11. "New Study: Kerry-Lieberman to Destroy up to 5.1 Million Jobs, Cost Families $1,042 per Year, Wealthiest Americans to Benefit," Institute for Energy Research, June 30, 2010 (emphasis in the original), www.institute forenergyresearch.org/2010/06/30/new-study-kerry-lieberman-to-destroy-up-to-5-1-million-jobs-cost-families-1042-per-year-wealthiest-americans-to-benefit/.

12. Declan McCullagh, "Obama Admin: Cap and Trade Could Cost Families $1,761 a Year," CBS News, September 15, 2009, www.cbsnews.com/8301-504383_162-5314040-504383.html.

13. "Paying President's 'Price on Carbon,'" ICECAP, June 30, 2010, http://ice cap.us/index.php/go/political-climate/paying_presidents_price_on_carbon/.

14. McCullagh, "Obama Admin: Cap and Trade Could Cost Families $1,761 a Year."

15. Amory Lovins, quoted in "The Plowboy Interview with Amory Lovins," Mother Earth News, November–December 1977, www.motherearthnews .com/Renewable-Energy/1977-11-01/Amory-Lovins.aspx?page=14. (Emphasis in the orginal.)

16. Paul Ehrlich, "An Ecologist's Perspective on Nuclear Power," *Federation of American Scientists Public Issue Report,* May–June 1978.

17. "Wind Power's Contribution to Electric Power Generation and Impact on Farms and Rural Communities," Report to the Ranking Democratic Member, Committee on Agriculture, Nutrition, and Forestry, U.S. Senate, September 2004, www.gao.gov/cgi-bin/getrpt?GAO-04-756.

18. "Renewable Energy Sources in the United States," Nationalatlas.gov, www. nationalatlas.gov/articles/people/a_energy.html#three/.

Chapter 10

1. Dave Foreman, quoted in Tamsin Osborne, "Eco-Problems of the 80s Return to Haunt Us," *New Scientist,* December 3, 2008 (posted in comments), www.newscientist.com/article/dn16189-ecoproblems-of-the-80s-return-to-haunt-us.html/.

2. James Lovelock, quoted in "Quotes from the Environmental Community: Understand Their Position and Philosophy," People for Preserving Our

Western Heritage, www.peopleforwesternheritage.com/PFWHRMAddi-tionalQuotes.htm.

3. James Lovelock, *Healing Gaia: Practical Medicine for the Planet* (New York: Harmony Books, 1991), 153.

4. Prince Philip, in a speech to the World Wildlife Fund, quoted in Edward Hooper, *The River* (New York: Little, Brown, 1999), 176.

5. John Davis, quoted in Osborne, "Eco-Problems of the 80s Return to Haunt Us."

6. Christopher Manes, quoted in "Environment, Eugenics Quotes," Climategate .TV, http://climategate.tv/?tag=new-world-order/.

7. David Brower, quoted in Rael Jean Isaac and Erich Isaac, *The Coercive Utopians* (Washington, D.C.: Regnery, 1985), 74.

8. Statement taken from *The First Global Revolution,* a 1993 study sponsored by the Club of Rome, quoted in Alexander King and Bertrand Schneider, *The First Global Revolution: A Report by the Council of the Club of Rome* (Hyderabad, India: Orient Longman, 1993), 75 (italics added).

9. Ervin Laszlo, quoted in "Club of Rome's World Government, Climate-Change and Depopulation Agenda Exposed," http://newworldorderreport. com/News/tabid/266/ID/28/Club-of-Romes-world-government-climate-change-and-depopulation-agenda-exposed.aspx/.

10. Michael Fox, quoted in William Perry Pendley, *The War on the West* (Washington, D.C.: Henry Regnery, 1995), 15. Echoing the sentiment of population control to save the planet is Maurice King, who stated, "Global Sustainability requires the deliberate quest of poverty, reduced resource consumption and set levels of mortality control." Maurice King, quoted in Alan Korwin, Page Nine, http://pagenine.typepad.com/page_nine/2009/06/environmental-hoax-proof.html/.

11. Paul W. Taylor, *Respect for Nature* (Princeton, NJ: Princeton University Press, 1989), 115.

12. V. H. Heywood, ed., *Global Biodiversity Assessment,* United Nations Environment Programme (Cambridge: Cambridge University Press, 1995).

13. Editorial, *The Economist* (UK), December 28, 1988, 1.

14. Paul Ehrlich, *The Population Bomb* (New York: Ballantine, 1968), xi, 166.

15. Bahgat Elnadi and Adel Rifaat, "Interview with Jacques-Yves Cousteau," *The UNESCO Courier*, November, 1991, 13, http://www.unesco.org/new/en/unesco-courier/archives/.

16. Victor J. Yannacone Jr., quoted in the *Congressional Record* as Serial No. 92-A of Hearings on Federal Pesticide Control Act of 1971, 266–67.

17. Published statement from the *Earth First! Journal,* quoted in Alan Pell Crawford and Art Levine, "Planet Stricken," *Vogue,* September 1989, 710.

18. David M. Graber, review of *The End of Nature,* by Bill McKibben, *Los Angeles Times Book Review,* October 22, 1989, 9.

19. David Foreman, quoted in "The Green Economy—A Global Economic Suicide Pact," The Green Agenda, www.green-agenda.com/neweconomy.html.

20. David Foreman, quoted in Tom McDonnell, "Technical Review of the Wildlands Project and How It Is Affecting the Management of State, Federal and Private Lands in the United States," Wildlands Project History, www.citizenreviewonline.org/april_2002/wildlands_project_history.htm.

21. The direct quotes attributed to David Foreman are taken from Tom McDonnell, "Technical Review of the Wildlands Project."

22. For more on this, see "The Wildlands Project and UN Convention on Biological Diversity Plan to Restore Biodiversity in the United States," Discerning the Times, www.discerningtoday.org/wildlands_map_of_us.htm.

Chapter 11

1. Michael Barone, "How Climate-Change Fanatics Corrupted Science," *Washington Examiner,* February 3, 2010, www.washingtonexaminer.com/politics/How-climate-change-fanatics-corrupted-science-83396362.html.

2. "EPA: Greenhouse Gases Threaten Public Health and the Environment," December 7, 2009, http://yosemite.epa.gov/opa/admpress.nsf/0/08D11A45 1131BCA585257685005BF252/.

3. See "Fortifying the Foundation: State of the Voluntary Carbon Markets 2009," Ecosystem Marketplace, http://ecosystemmarketplace.com/documents/cms_documents/StateOfTheVoluntaryCarbonMarkets_2009.pdf.

4. Todd Wynn, "The Climate Swindle," *Oregon Catalyst*, April 9, 2010, www.oregoncatalyst.com/index.php/archives/3165-The-Climate-Swindle.html/.

5. Bruce Nussbaum, "Al Gore's Carbon Footprint Is Big," *Bloomberg Businessweek*, February 27, 2007, www.businessweek.com/innovate/NussbaumOn Design/archives/2007/02/gores_carbon_fo.html.

6. Bjorn Lomborg, *Cool It* (New York: Alfred A. Knopf, 2007), 42, 162.

7. Lomborg, *Cool It*, 47–48.

8. Marni Soupcoff, "Patrick Moore on Where Greenpeace Has It Wrong: Chlorine, Forests, Genetic Modification and Nuclear Energy," *National Post* (Ontario), May 12, 2008, http://network.nationalpost.com/np/blogs/fullcomment/archive/2008/05/12/patrick-moore-on-where-greenpeace-has-it-wrong-chlorine-forests-genetic-modification-and-nuclear-energy.aspx#ixzz0yDmxOavJ.

9. Michael Crichton, quoted in Global Warming Hysteria, May 4, 2010, www.globalwarminghysteria.com/environmentalism-as-religion-/.

10. Marc Morano, "Weather Channel Climate Expert Calls for Decertifying Global Warming Skeptics," *Inhofe EPW Press Blog*, January 17, 2007, http://epw.senate.gov/public/index.cfm?FuseAction=PressRoom.Blogs&Content Record_id=32abc0b0-802a-23ad-440a-88824bb8e528/.

11. Dave Roberts, "The Denial Industry," Grist, September 19, 2006, www.grist.org/article/the-denial-industry/.

12. Scott Pelley, *60 Minutes*, CBS, March 26, 2006. See also Brian Montopoli, "Scott Pelley and Catherine Herrick on Global Warming Coverage," *CBS News Blogs*, www.cbsnews.com/8301-500486_162-1431768-500486.html.

13. Al Gore, quoted in Roy W. Spencer, *Climate Confusion* (New York: Encounter Books, 2009), 94.

14. Richard Cizik, quoted in Paul Rogat Loeb, "Jesus and Climate Change: The Journey of Evangelical Leader Rich Cizik," Grist, April 27, 2010, www.grist

.org/article/2010-04-27-jesus-climate-change-journey-of-evangelical-leader-rich-cizik/.

15. Richard Lindzen, quoted in Marc Morano, "Meteorologist Likens Fear of Global Warming to 'Religious Belief,'" George C. Marshall Institute, December 2, 2004, www.marshall.org/article.php?id=265/.

16. Nigel Lawson, "The Economics of Climate Change: An Appeal to Reason," Centre for Policy Studies, November 1, 2006, www.cps.org.uk/cps_catalog/CPS_assets/579_ProductPreviewFile.pdf, page 16.

17. J. R. Dunn, "A Necessary Apocalypse," *American Thinker,* February 2, 2007, www.americanthinker.com/2007/02/a_necessary_apocalypse.html.

18. Malachi Martin, *The Keys of This Blood* (New York: Simon and Schuster, 1990), 258–60.

19. Martin, *The Keys of This Blood,* 364.

20. Martin, *The Keys of This Blood,* 259.

21. Al Gore, *Earth in the Balance* (New York: Houghton Mifflin, 1992), 265.

22. Gore, *Earth in the Balance,* 273.

23. Gore, *Earth in the Balance,* 264.

Chapter 12

1. Ronald Bailey, "Royal Society to Re-Evaluate Position on Global Warming," *Reason,* June 1, 2010, http://reason.com/blog/2010/06/01/royal-society-to-re-evaluate-p/.

2. Sir Alan Rudge, quoted in Ben Webster, "Rebel Scientists Force Royal Society to Accept Climate Change Scepticism," *Times* (London), May 29, 2010, www.timesonline.co.uk/tol/news/environment/article7139407.ece.

3. Kenneth Green, "A Death Spiral for Climate Alarmism, Redux?" Master-Resource, September 30, 2009, www.masterresource.org/2009/09/a-death-spiral-for-climate-alarmism-the-dynamics-of-a-fading-unsolvable-alarm/.

4. Stefan Theil, "Uncertain Science," *Newsweek,* May 28, 2010, www.newsweek.com/2010/05/28/uncertain-science.html.

5. Mike Hulme and Martin Mahony, "Climate Change: What Do We Know About the IPCC?" *Progress in Physical Geography* 34, no. 5 (October 2010): 10–11, http://mikehulme.org/wp-content/uploads/2010/01/Hulme-Mahony-PiPG.pdf.

6. Global Warming Petition Project, www.petitionproject.org/.

7. Coby Beck, "How to Talk to a Climate Sceptic," hosted by the World Wildlife Fund as "How to Answer the Claims of a Climate Change Sceptic," http://wwf.panda.org/about_our_earth/aboutcc/cause/climate_sceptics/.

8. Juliette Jowit, "France and Japan Propose an 'IPCC for Nature,'" *Guardian* (UK), June 9, 2010, www.guardian.co.uk/environment/2010/jun/09/france-japan-ipcc-for-nature/.

9. For more on the multi-decadal oscillations, see David Rose, "The Mini Ice Age Starts Here," *Mail Online* (UK), January 10, 2010, www.dailymail.co.uk/sciencetech/article-1242011/DAVID-ROSE-The-mini-ice-age-starts-here.html#ixzz0yENLhE84/.

10. Mojib Latif, quoted in "Inhofe Calls 2009 the Year of the Skeptic in Senate Floor Speech," U.S. Senate Committee on Environment and Public Works, November 18, 2009, http://epw.senate.gov/public/index.cfm?FuseAction=Minority.PressReleases&ContentRecord_id=0a725d63-802a-23ad-44ea-01cf57e06fb7/.

11. David Derbyshire, "The World Could Get Colder over the Next Two Decades—But Still Hotter in the Long Run, Expert Predicts," *Mail Online* (UK), September 10, 2009, www.dailymail.co.uk/sciencetech/article-1212442/The-world-colder-decades--hotter-long-run-expert-predicts.html#ixzz0yEeoJ3tP/.

SELECTED BIBLIOGRAPHY

Booker, Christopher. *The Real Global Warming Disaster.* New York: Continuum International, 2009.

Horner, Christopher C. *Red Hot Lies.* Washington, D.C.: Regnery, 2008.

Klaus, Václav. *Blue Planet in Green Shackles.* Washington, D.C.: Competitive Enterprise Institute, 2008.

Levitt, Steven D., and Stephen J. Dubner. *Super Freakonomics.* Toronto: Harper Collins, 2009.

Lomborg, Bjorn. *Cool It.* New York: Alfred A. Knopf, 2007.

Plimer, Ian. *Heaven and Earth.* Lanham, MD: Taylor Trade, 2009.

Singer, S. Fred, and Dennis T. Avery. *Unstoppable Global Warming.* Lanham, MD: Rowman and Littlefield, 2008.

Spencer, Roy W. *Climate Confusion.* New York: Encounter Books, 2009.

Sussman, Brian. *Climategate.* Washington, D.C.: WND Books, 2010.

Printed in the United States
by Baker & Taylor Publisher Services